Baudrillard Now

Baudrillard Now

Current Perspectives in Baudrillard Studies

**EDITED BY
RYAN BISHOP**

polity

This English-language edition copyright © Polity Press 2009

This edition published in 2009 by Polity Press. Originally published in the People's Republic of China by Henan University Press. Published by arrangement with Henan University Press.

"Pursuit in Paris" was first published in *Cultural Politics*, Volume 4, Number 2, July 2008. The author gratefully acknowledges permission from Berg Publications to reprint the article in this collection.
A shorter version of "Baudrillard and the Evil Genius" appeared in *Theory, Culture and Society* (Sage).
A modified section of "Baudrillard, Death and Cold War Theory" appeared in *Social Identities* (Taylor and Francis).

The right of the authors to be identified as Author of this Work has been asserted in accordance with the UK Copyright, Designs and Patents Act 1988.

Polity Press
65 Bridge Street
Cambridge CB2 1UR, UK

Polity Press
350 Main Street
Malden, MA 02148, USA

ISBN-13: 978-0-7456-4707-4
ISBN-13: 978-0-7456-4708-1(pb)

A catalogue record for this book is available from the British Library.

Typeset in 11 on 13 pt Bembo by
Servis Filmsetting Limited, Stockport, Cheshire.
Printed and bound by MPG Books Group, UK

The publisher has used its best endeavours to ensure that the URLs for external websites referred to in this book are correct and active at the time of going to press. However, the publisher has no responsibility for the websites and can make no guarantee that a site will remain live or that the content is or will remain appropriate.

Every effort has been made to trace all copyright holders, but if any have been inadvertently overlooked the publishers will be pleased to include any necessary credits in any subsequent reprint or edition.

For further information on Polity, visit our website: www.politybooks.com

Contents

Notes on Contributors

JOHN ARMITAGE teaches media and communication at Northumbria University, UK. He is co-editor, with Ryan Bishop and Douglas Kellner, of the Berg journal *Cultural Politics*.

JOHN BECK teaches English and American literature at Newcastle University. He is the author of *Writing the Radical Center: William Carlos Williams, John Dewey, and American Cultural Politics* (SUNY, 2001) and *Dirty Wars: Landscape, Power, and Waste in Western American Literature* (Nebraska, 2009), and co-editor of *American Visual Cultures* (Continuum, 2005)

RYAN BISHOP teaches at the National University of Singapore and has published on critical theory, military technology, avant-garde aesthetics, urbanism, architecture, literature, and international sex tourism. He edits or serves on the editorial boards of several journals. In addition to other works, he is co-author with John Phillips of *Modernist Avant-Garde Aesthetics and Contemporary Military Technology: Technicities of Perception* (Edinburgh University Press, 2010).

DOUGLAS KELLNER is George Kneller Chair in the Philosophy of Education at UCLA and is author of many books on social theory, politics, history, and culture, including *Critical Theory, Marxism, and Modernity* and *Jean Baudrillard: From Marxism to Postmodernism and Beyond*; works in cultural studies such as *Media Culture* and *Media Spectacle*; a trilogy of books on postmodern theory with Steve Best; and a trilogy of books on the media and the Bush administration, encompassing *Grand Theft 2000, From 9/11 to Terror War*, and *Media Spectacle and the Crisis of Democracy*. Kellner's *Guys and Guns Amok: Domestic Terrorism and School Shootings from the Oklahoma City Bombings to the Virginia Tech Massacre* won the 2008 AESA award as the best book on education. Forthcoming in 2009 with Blackwell is Kellner's *Cinema Wars: Hollywood Film and Politics in the Bush/Cheney Era*. His website is at http://www.gseis. ucla.edu/faculty/kellner/kellner.html.

JOHN W. P. PHILLIPS teaches in the Department of English at the National University of Singapore. He has published on philosophy, literature, critical theory, psychoanalysis, aesthetics, military technology, urbanism, and Asian cities. Along with Ryan Bishop, Mike Featherstone, and Couze Venn, he is one of the editors of the *New Encyclopaedia Project* (volume I: *Problematizing Global Knowledge*; volume II (in preparation): *Megacities: Problematizing the Urban*). He is the co-author, with Ryan Bishop, of a forthcoming book on modernist aesthetics and military technology. He has just completed a manuscript on Jacques Derrida and is currently researching a project on autoimmunity in biotechnology and political philosophy.

MARK POSTER is Chair of the Department of Film and Media Studies and a member of the History Department at the University of California, Irvine. He has a courtesy appointment in the Department of Comparative Literature. He is a member of the Critical Theory Institute. His recent books are: *Information Please: Culture and Politics in a Digital Age* (Duke University Press, 2006); *What's the Matter with the Internet?: A Critical Theory of Cyberspace* (University of Minnesota Press, 2001); *The Information Subject* in Critical Voices Series (New York: Gordon and Breach Arts International, 2001); *Cultural History and Postmodernity* (New York: Columbia University Press, 1997); *The Second Media Age* (London: Polity and New York: Blackwell, 1995); and *The Mode of Information* (London: Blackwell and Chicago: University of Chicago Press, 1990).

Acknowledgments

Although books are written in isolation, they are never written alone. The case is rendered all the more literal with an edited collection such as this one, and it provides me great joy and humility to express my gratitude and pleasure to numerous individuals and institutions without whom this volume would not exist. First and foremost, I would like to thank my dear friends and colleagues whose work appears in the collection. Professor Jin Huimin of the Chinese Academy of Social Sciences, Prof. Yunpeng Zhang of Henan University Press, and Dai Abao, my sterling translator, deserve special thanks for suggesting a book on Baudrillard for the Chinese market that went through several transformations from English to Chinese and Chinese to English to become this book. The Dean's office of the Faculty of Arts and Social Sciences at the National University of Singapore provided research grants that helped realize the volume; a special debt is owed to Robbie Goh, Tan Tai Yong and Lily Kong, scholars and administrators without peer. The faculty members and graduate students that participate in the Science, Technology and Society research cluster at NUS contributed invaluable intellectual input and stimulation. Thanks too to all the wonderful scholars working on Jean Baudrillard for such inspiring engagements. Numerous friends kindly gave of their time and ideas, and some deserve special thanks: Greg Clancey, Li Shiqiao, Mike Featherstone, Couze Venn, Ingrid Hoofd, Michael M. J. Fischer, Tania Roy, Chris Turner, Sean Cubitt, and my colleagues at *Cultural Politics* and *Theory, Culture & Society*. Many thanks to all the terrific people at Polity, especially Clare Ansell and Jonathan Skerrett, who made this a painless process, and most importantly Andrea Drugan, a dream of an editor if ever there was one. For their endless love, patience, and sarcastic asides, my deepest gratitude to and for my family near and far: my father Steve, my brothers Eric and Steve, my daughters Sarah and Sophia, and my loveliest collaborator Adeline; it is to them that this book is dedicated.

Introduction: The End of Baudrillard and Beyond

Ryan Bishop

The perfect symbol of the end of the century is (or was rather) the numerical clock at the Beaubourg (Centre Georges Pompidou) in Paris. There, the race against time was measured in millions of seconds. The Beaubourg clock illustrates the reversal of time characteristic of our contemporary modernity. Time is no longer counted from its point of origin, as a progressive succession. It is rather subtracted from the end (5, 4, 3, 2, 1, 0). It is like a bomb with delayed effect. The end of time is no longer the symbolic completion of history, but the mark of a possible fatigue, of a regressive countdown. We are no longer living according to a projected vision of progress or production. The final illusion of history has disappeared since history is now encapsulated in a numerical countdown (just as the final illusion of humankind disappears when man is encapsulated in genetic computations). Counting the seconds from now to the end means that the end is near, that one has already gone beyond the end.

Jean Baudrillard (1998)

The problem is, rather, that of a precession of thought over the event – and yet, simultaneously, of the precession of the event over thought. It's this double helix that's mysterious. In the case of the World Trade Center, for example, everything I've been writing for twenty years was, ultimately, something like a prefigured shock wave of the event, as though it had always been there, identified in a kind of retrospective anticipation. Thought's neither a prophecy nor a prediction. It's a prefiguration. It's already there like the event in a sense, and it finds its fulfilment in something that wholly escapes it. The event impacts on thought even before it has occurred. And when it finally happens, it's both the realization of thought and its end.

Jean Baudrillard and Enrique Valiente Noailles (2007: 4)

To call a book *Baudrillard Now* risks hubris or tautology – perhaps both. For Baudrillard has always been writing "the now" and is never more current than he is right now. But to say that Baudrillard has been, always was and always is, writing about the current moment is more than slightly glib and glosses over the many diverse and complex ways the present appears and disappears from view in his work in the guise of origins, history, time in general, and most specifically "the end": our being consumed by as well as our consumption of the end, of endings, and the drive for completion. The *topos* called "the end" – its illusion, impossibility, necessity, desirability, and horror – winds its way through almost every single piece in this volume just as it finds many manifestations in Baudrillard's work. So it is wise to begin with the end. Applying Baudrillard's continued interest in reversibility, we can paraphrase Groucho Marx as Captain Spaulding and ventriloquize for Baudrillard: "I just left to say I must be staying."

Baudrillard is, amongst other things, a philosopher of ends and a theorist of eschatologies, which imply in themselves origins and teleologies, all of which Baudrillard would eschew while nonetheless studying them rigorously. His is an apocalyptic vision of sorts but one without revelation, as Jacques Derrida noted in another related context. The end of humanity Baudrillard spies on the horizon is built into the historical trends he analyzes, especially those that constitute his late concept "integral reality." Teleologies are always also eschatologies, trajectories with ready-made terminals. The drive for completion, to end everything, marks our twenty-first century as much as it did the latter half of the twentieth, the twilight of which we occupy in shadowy uncertainty. The idea of ends, especially the end of history, is an illusion, a creation of metaphysical thought, but one that lingers and refuses to go away. Its staying power thus explains our fixation on origins, which in turn explain the teleologies that render legible the rational, purposeful design of the straight path from origins to ends. Baudrillard's death in 2007, which seems more present and current now than it did at the time, is an event present in or the subtext of many of the chapters in this collection. Perhaps this explains one of the reasons that Baudrillard as a philosopher of ends remains so purposefully at play now in this collection. From the critical re-examinations of Baudrillard's oeuvre offered by Douglas Kellner and Ryan Bishop and John Phillips through the pieces by John Beck and Kellner, and concluding appropriately with Phillips on humanity's end, the book gathers some of the many threads of thought on ends and endings found in Baudrillard's writings to create an arbitrarily arranged engagement with the illusions and seductions operating in eschatologies across various topics and texts.

Phillips starts his chapter with a quotation from Baudrillard's last full work to appear in English, *The Intelligence of Evil*, discussing the import of the impossibility and necessity of ending for "the human" and humanity: "The human race owes its becoming (and perhaps even its survival) entirely to the fact that it had no end in itself, and certainly not that of becoming what it is (of fulfilling itself, identifying with itself)" (Baudrillard, 2005: 212). Using this statement, especially the provocative dimensions of the phrase "no end in itself," Phillips addresses Baudrillard's recasting of Hegel's concepts of *Ansich* (itself a reworking of the Greek terms *potentia* and *dúnamis*) as "the end in itself" and *Fürsich* (which revises the Greek *actus* and *enérgeia*) as "the not yet" in relation to Hegelian constructions of teleology and history. Phillips argues that

> Baudrillard understands history, as if in a technical revision of Hegel's teleology, as the intensification over hundreds of years of the domination in Western societies of spurious and superficial abstractions that stand in for reality. He describes this intensification in terms of "successive mutations of the law of value." Here we may recognize a kind of abstraction that can acknowledge its own force of simulation. Baudrillard's brand of simulation is produced, with meticulous

attention to the details of historical becoming, in order to combat an overwhelming trend, which seems mobilized to reduce the forces of simulation or to deny them even as it manifests those forces to the greatest imaginable extent.

The connections between various kinds of end or ending and simulation reside in the many technologies of information, calculation and homogenization that are all that we have "after the end," an impossible ending that we have already moved through. Yet for all of Baudrillard's seemingly bleak perspectives on the fate of the human in the face of these forces that we have generated and applied to ourselves and that allow us to move between the false origin of fossils and the false end of cloning, we have reason to find some comfort in the irresolvable clash of the horror of completion and our utter failure to complete. This state of affairs is neatly summed up by Phillips when he asserts that

> When reading Baudrillard, it is not possible to avoid the sense that we members of the twenty-first century are unlucky to live in a world dominated by the drive for completion, and which attacks us on multiple levels. Nonetheless Baudrillard can best be characterized, alongside his eternal vigilance against completion, by his affirmation of the essential indeterminacy of a future whose becoming belongs to an irreducible "in itself," a potential that knows no end. In a world whose business it is to anticipate the future we should expect monsters; but to affirm the chance of an indeterminate future is to welcome that possibility.

If Phillips discusses Baudrillard's thoughts about the metaphysical necessity of ends for humanity, then Beck uses the Charlton Heston character, Taylor, from *Planet of the Apes* to remind us that the last man in America is also the last man for humanity. Taylor's end of humanity is the embodiment of all ends that are the American project. Taylor is the unwitting astronaut of Reagan's America just as Baudrillard himself is the cognizant astronaut of Reagan's America as written up in Baudrillard's own *America*. The operating assumptions of Reaganite triumphalism that Baudrillard finds himself positioned within during his US sojourn articulate a perfection that allows no resistance and that contains nothing outside itself: a vision of the US as the perfect realization of all systems, calculations and material acquisition. Ever the protean rhetorician, Baudrillard performs his critique by occupying Taylor's discourse as well as Reagan's. Similarly he takes up that of various critics and celebrants of the US within the stock division of historical Old World–New World typologies. Countering critics who charged Baudrillard with an unthinking lazy repetition of European criticisms of and clichés about US culture, Beck explains that the occupation of these rhetorical domains consciously renders Baudrillard

> the last man, self-positioned as outside the society he has "discovered." What has come true for Taylor is that the monstrous other world he believes he has been arbitrarily flung into is in fact the product of his own world and his values: he is not lost but has been at home all along. "It is the American way of life," Baudrillard argues, a way of life Europeans think is "naive or culturally worthless," that will in fact offer a "graphic representation of the end of our values" (Baudrillard 1988: 98). The horror in *America* is that Baudrillard, like Taylor in *Planet of the Apes*, discovers that he speaks the same language as the awful future society he has encountered.

The end of our values, then, is found in and made possible through the end of the possibility of another language with which to speak of cultural values, existential realization or, even, ends. Beck extends this point by arguing that *America* "speaks in a language – the American language of incarnational freedom – that it does not fully understand, like a phonetic language. Or, perhaps more accurately, it speaks a language that has been learned through reading and watching rather than through conversation." Linking Baudrillard's work on simulation to that of the US-incarnated rhetoric, Beck claims that neither one has an outside, and both bespeak their all-smothering inclusiveness. The end of alternative thought and language is found here.

In Beck, we find Baudrillard as Taylor – the last man, or in other words "the American" – engaging the end of language. In Phillips we get the end of humanity in the endless calculation of futural possibility that destroys the end as end. With Kellner's brief meditation on the very late essay by Baudrillard entitled "On Disappearance," we have the more dire possibility: complete human disappearance. Kellner quotes the essay's opening "dramatic invocation: 'Let us speak then of the world from which human beings have disappeared.'" Reworking the terrain of the dialectic between appearance and disappearance important to Baudrillard's thought, Kellner suggests the article also returns to a number of Baudrillard's motifs: "the disappearance of the real, the subject, and the human being itself in a world of simulation, hyperreality, virtual reality, networks, and the system of what Baudrillard calls 'integral reality.'" The disappearance of the real, though not necessarily its end, initiates the fatal process of the disappearance of humans from the world. Once again, language plays a central role in these disappearances. Although the intensification of technologies of disappearance is an idea he shares with Paul Virilio, the relationship of language to disappearance is a point that Baudrillard takes from Hegel. "On Disappearance" picks up a theme also found in *Exiles from Dialogue* as well as other later pieces by Baudrillard: that once something is named or represented as a concept then we have begun to hasten its doom. The mere act of language use initiates the disappearance of that which it brings into being through the sleight of hand that is representation.

To press this point a bit more, advertising would exacerbate further the disappearance begun by language and naming several fold. Thus if any further proof were required for the disappearance and end of humanity, one would only need look at the recent (2008) campaign designed for Dow Chemical company that reads: "Humanity is the world's most precious natural resource."[1] The ad includes a mock periodic table symbol "Hu" and an attendant periodical number. Placed under the sign of chemistry and the taxonomic neatness of the periodic table (all within an ad), humanity disappears into resource: a thought that demands a nod toward Martin Heidegger. The larger campaign ad, in a conceit reminiscent of John Donne, concentrates on "the human element." The lines and graphics suggest that more than just the human body exists as a source for mining, extrapolation, and exploitation: humanity in and of itself does. In an age fixated on counting down time, racing toward ecological and environmental exhaustion, and waging wars for precious natural resources (i.e. finding our ends in fossils), then the evocation of humanity as yet another dwindling resource in need of preserving, maximizing, and husbanding stamps the human and humanity as near-extinct entities whose bones might foreshadow another revival of energetic activity just as the demise of the dinosaurs did for us. The shadow of the Bhopal disaster falls across the ad in many ways, not the least of which being that the child featured as the hope of humanity's future clearly comes from "the developing world" as his attire indicates. The corporation mines the grisly petrochemical disaster for indications of hope just as Western culture seeks solace in the flashes of the human spirit displayed in distant catastrophe. But just as human rights signal the end of the human in the global order of Integral Reality, so the corporation's advertising copy and graphics signal the increasing abstraction of objects upon which the economic orders of Integral Reality operate, thus hastening our collective end. In case we feel a turn to metaphysics might salvage us, the Dow ad has anticipated that move too, and it also includes the line "the future is now." The present too disappears into a projected and predicted future just as the future and the past – not to mention space – disappear in the grips of "real time" and the technologies that render it ever-present.

Several chapters contained in this collection provide doublings and extensions of Baudrillard's thought by bringing aspects of his work explicitly into dialogue with that of another thinker (as Phillips does with Hegel) especially as they pertain to the status of objects and their relation to simulation and the hyperreal. In each instance, the chapters by John Armitage, Mark Poster, and Bishop and Phillips take leads from Baudrillard's writing, extend them in various directions, address the imperatives contained in his increasingly productive analyses and return to the concepts with variations, modifications, and contradictions.

Armitage's "Pursuit in Paris" uses the positive phenomenology of Alphonso Lingis to place Baudrillard's "revenge of the object" in creative tension over the shifting status of subject–object relations within cultural theory. Taking Baudrillard's conceit of reversibility as it pertains to standard Western notions of subject–object relations and his provocative assertions about the object playing with (and occasionally exacting revenge on) the subject, Armitage uses Lingis's imperative of the object that calls us forth, outside of ourselves, to engage with a world that speaks to us directly through the senses. Thus the senses are fully and (non-)prosthetically engaged in Armitage's photo chapter. They lead him and his partner in a guided pursuit of Baudrillard's grave. Because the chapter is shot through with Baudrillard and Lingis, this pursuit is by no means grim, but rather thoughtfully and gratefully embodied and sensuous in ways both thinkers guide us toward. But there is clearly no resolution possible between Lingis and Baudrillard insofar as the object goes. For Lingis, the object is immediately, directly, and unavoidably accessible in a neo-Romantic, phenomenological manner while such unmediated access for Baudrillard is absurd. In both instances, the object takes on an imperative but does so for very different reasons and ends. It is this tension and the demands of it on cultural and visual theory that Armitage undertakes in order to consider how Baudrillard's work might, in Armitage's words, be "conserved, sheltered, restored, and, crucially, developed." (Once again, the ending of Baudrillard proves impossible.)

This oblique homage to Baudrillard's "Pursuit in Venice" and his writings on Sophie Calle's *La Suite vénitienne* invites consideration of the medium of photography: part of Baudrillard's own artistic ground. The photographic images that punctuate Armitage's chapter also punctuate the ruminations on the object conducted by Lingis and Baudrillard, directing us to the deeply paradoxical nature of the photographic image as the site where the object becomes both most apparent and most attenuated, both most easily grasped and most elusive. Photography reveals, as Baudrillard points out, how "technical equipment and the world enter into collusion; 'objective' technology and the potency of the object converge" (Baudrillard, 2001: 139). Baudrillard actually posits "a rough and ready phenomenology" rather close to that enacted by Armitage, one that could bring Lingis and Baudrillard together if only for a brief uncomfortable moment. This phenomenology is found in the subversive function of the photographic image when it "becomes literal" thus creating "a phenomenology of absence which is usually impossible, because the object is normally occulted by the subject" (140–1). He likens this to what is called the "apophatic," which in theology provides a methodology of knowing what God is by "what He is not" (142). Similarly we know the world and the object by what they are not, "showing it up through what is cut away" like a cameo or conversely an intaglio (142). Armitage's chapter carves away both Baudrillard's and Lingis's theories of objects with text and photographs that allow them to shine through in a negative (as in a photograph) fashion. The photographic image, for Baudrillard, becomes the quintessential site for the object's literalness, disappearance, and reassertion. "The photographic act is a duel: that is to say it is a challenge to the object and the object's defiance of that challenge," he writes. "Where that confrontation is ignored, there can only be escape into technology and aesthetics – that is to say, into the most facile of solutions" (146).

Mark Poster continues the discussion of the escape into technology and aesthetics but as anything other than a facile solution, though his media object of exploration at first glance appears to be amongst the most facile of all broadcast ephemera. Using Baudrillard's notion of hyperreality and Foucault's "hermeneutics of the self" to read "reality TV" shows, Poster's contribution to the volume argues that the contestants on shows in which they undergo cosmetic surgery are engaged in a kind of updated and thoroughly (but knowingly) mediated "care of the self." In the process, he reveals a variation of the hyperreal that includes a more sustained theory of the body than one finds in most of Baudrillard's writings. His chapter asserts that reading Baudrillard and Foucault together through the lens of these reality TV shows allows each to address what he perceives to a be a lack in the other: "Baudrillard's lack of a theory of the body and Foucault's treatment of mediation without a theory of media."

The objects Poster examines include their appearances and operations at various levels of mediation, simulation, and virtuality, including the body, techniques of the body, the self, reality TV shows, cosmetic surgery, body art performed through cosmetic surgery, and popular culture aesthetics. Their status as objects leads to a mediation through media that Baudrillard refers to as a "fractal subject" existing both within television and without. Resisting a too doggedly deterministic reading of the influence of reality TV as a form of neoliberal domination that further dupes or exploits the masses, Poster argues that the participants who experience cosmetic surgery on these shows are engaging in an updated care of the self that is neither "liberatory [n]or resistant" but which nonetheless allows them to explore possibilities of subject fashioning "in the current formation of mediate culture." And this position presses forward ways of understanding the hyperreal that both reinforce and deviate from Baudrillard's. The technological access allowed the audience to the operations that patients/contestants undergo, coupled with the carefully edited formats of the shows, brings viewers closer to the events while simultaneously further distancing them. In a very Baudrillardian statement, Poster claims that in the current moment "information machines are central to the human experience" and that "the determination of what is private and what is public is fundamentally configured by the role of information machines in everyday life." The hyperreal emerges as one of the main effects and causes of the interactions between humans and information machines. This interaction or interface provides the extension of Foucault's techniques of care of the self into the domain of communication media – a space Foucault largely ignores except for minor gestures toward the technology of writing. No longer tangential to the processes and techniques operative in the care of the self, information machines are now requisite for its realization as the fractal self negotiates the private/public divide constituted, mediated, and undermined by these same machines.

Bishop and Phillips also take up the connections between technology and aesthetics when they pose the eponymous question of their chapter "What is a Tank?" In the process of exploring answers to that question, they use the psychoanalytic work of Wilfred Bion and the innovative artistic appropriations of Constable by contemporary artist Chris Dobrowolski to address Baudrillard's notions of simulation, the hyperreal, and Integral Reality insofar as they are each concerned with projection and defense. The chapter uses aesthetics to link two concerns: one, the possibility of critical responsibility and engagement in current technological and political environments; and two, the structure and history of technology and technological thinking that underpin these current conditions. Similarly the tank acts as a hinge between Baudrillard's writings on Integral Reality and hyperreality, and Bion's psychoanalytic work on the conditions of experience as resulting from developmental attitudes to and defenses against sensation. Bringing Baudrillard into conversation with Bion, as with the pieces by Armitage and Poster just discussed, extends and doubles some of Baudrillard's notions of simulation and hyperreality by exploring how they function within, and as, military technology interacting with aesthetics and our conceptualization of thought.

The tank becomes literally and figuratively a vehicle for Bion's theories about the senses and how thought develops in relation to the contradictory impulses of intensifying and nullifying sensate experience. Bion's treatment of traumatized World War I soldiers led to psychoanalytic work that anticipates Baudrillard's writings about the merging of biophysioanatomical sciences in that he conceived early on what we now recognize as the prosthetic nature of human sensation and its relation to cognition – what Derrida would call "prosthetics at the origin." Bishop and Phillips argue that

> Bion's theoretical discussions help to complicate distinctions between classical functionalism (the notion of the machine as an extension of the natural body or psyche) and what Baudrillard calls mortal "deconstruction": the "extension of death" that the body undergoes when its parts merge with, or are confused with, machine parts (as in his reading of J. G. Ballard's *Crash* from *Simulation and Simulacra*). Bion does not talk of lost unity (which Baudrillard believes still remains the horizon of psychoanalysis) but rather he talks, like Baudrillard himself, of psychic experience built out of disparate sensations through kinds of *projection* and *defense*. The notion of *projection* central to both thinkers (Bion's *projective identification* and Baudrillard's *three orders of simulacra*) serves as a kind of catastrophic mediation that "middles" rather than mediates.

Through this catastrophic mediation or middling, the energetic extension of the self operating in and through its various tele-technologies found in Bion is transformed and subdued in the suffocatingly claustrophobic unifying power of Integral Reality.

We are left with nothing other than total immersion in hyperreality, where, to quote Baudrillard, "the equally routinized violence of war" is compounded by "the equally routinized violence of the images" (Baudrillard, 2005: 77). The image is clearly a site of violence, challenge, and duel, just as much as language is in Baudrillard's writings. Beck's concentration on the rhetoric and language of Baudrillard's work reveals another important theme running throughout the pieces in this collection. Baudrillard's prodigious skills as a writer are well documented, and his capacity for intensifying ambiguities resident in language as well as for poetic evocation and compression lend his work both its artful ingenuity and its potential as a target for too-easy dismissal as postmodern doggerel. Though infinitely quotable, Baudrillard's aphoristic writing (a stylistic move he borrows from Nietzsche but obviously filtered through Holderlin, Mallarme, and Baudelaire) has the capacity to seem unsystematic and sustained in its engagement with philosophical issues. "The enigma of meaning," Baudrillard says, "is the secret of writing, and this is expressed in its concision and its aphoristic form" (Baudrillard and Noailles, 2007: 12). But interpreting Baudrillard's style as unsystematic and unrigorous is a mistake that can only result from not reading him carefully, as many of the pieces in this volume indicate repeatedly. (The critical overview by Kellner and that by Bishop and Phillips discuss this point at length). The very elasticity of language combined with a rigor of development and connections between ideas over time and many publications, the constant upping of the rhetorical stakes and escalation of lexical and categorical terms, is in fact what gives Baudrillard's writing its cumulative power and its sustained engagement with conditions of thought, experience, and action. Simultaneously language, as does the object, manifests itself as a remarkable exemplar of reversibility and duality: able to think us as easily as we are able to think it, which at some level is a bit of a hoary chestnut. However, Baudrillard takes us further, into territory that is familiar to scholars of Jacques Derrrida, by insisting that we are never freed from language's obligation or its form although its obligation and form are what allow us freedom to think and write (Baudrillard and Noailles, 2007: 10–11). In this manner, Baudrillard updates ideas found in the hermeneutical work of the

German idealists, some of whom he read in his youth, while also invoking elements of German Romanticism. Several chapters in this collection take a direct cue from Baudrillard by dent of inhabiting discourses and working them from the inside. This is an often-overlooked aspect of Baudrillard's own writing, one which functions almost as a free indirect discourse of parodic ventriloquization: what we might call a pataphysics of poesis. (One is reminded of Jarry's profligate borrowings from scientific journals and books when building his collaged "physics beyond metaphysics.") Beck's chapter provides the most extended and explicit example of this rhetorical move in its working through of the various discursive domains that Baudrillard brings into analytic play and which have been a site for the short-sighted criticism of Baudrillard's *America*. Beck shows how Baudrillard occupies these discursive domains to explore the ways they configure our understanding of America and its understanding of itself regardless of what the cultural and political processes within the nation-state might be. The insularity of these discourses, not to mention their capacity for squelching resistance or alternatives to them, suffocates experience before it has a chance to emerge, thus predetermining Europe's engagement with America and America's with itself. Beck's analysis provides an insightful engagement with Baudrillard's rhetoric as well as life-long fascination with rhetoric's effects on our understanding of the world.

The chapter by Bishop, "Baudrillard, Death, and Cold War Theory," also uses Baudrillard's appropriation of Cold War rhetoric, lexical items, conceptual apparatuses, and technologies to argue that they are of a piece inseparable from one another, just as the chapter itself occupies exactly the same discursive and rhetorical terrain. Arguing Baudrillard's significance as a Cold War theorist from inside the Cold War means that Baudrillard's rhetoric when addressing systems and technologies designed to end the world comes from those very systems and technologies as well as their attendant discursive formations. His language and thought, in other words, co-opts those deployed by eschatology's engineers. Just as Cold War discursive and surveillance practices were occupied with the ways in which the local informed and influenced the global ("We defend every place," Douglas MacArthur infamously

said) as well as vice versa, Baudrillard's writing always reflects how
the whole can be found in the part and the part in the whole
but without the circuit being capable of closure despite its being
designed to do so and its desires to do so.

The contribution from Armitage similarly amounts to a sustained
and strategic set of reflected and refracted discursive elements borrowed from both Lingis and Baudrillard. Readers can find deftly
woven throughout the text allusions and snippets of paraphrases
and oblique quotes from the two theorists at odds with each other
insofar as the basic premises of the chapter operate. The piece
reads in places as if Armitage armed with a tape recorder had been
running down a hallway in which two almost exclusive discussions of the status of the sign and the object (one led by Lingis and
the other by Baudrillard) were taking place in the rooms he flew
past. Thus Armitage becomes a squatter in two barely overlapping
camps and puts their languages in play with one another. In this
sense most specifically, the piece continues an important dimension of Baudrillard's rhetoric: the ability to dwell within a discourse
while simultaneously extending and undermining it from within
its own terms and on its own conditions.

The structure of this collection reveals its desire to address
multiple but not necessarily exclusive audiences. The two critical
overview chapters of Baudrillard's career – the ones by Kellner and
Bishop and Phillips that lead off the book – speak to readers from
a range of levels of familiarity with Baudrillard and critical theory:
from those just starting out in the field to those well-traveled within
it. The remaining chapters exemplify but a sliver of the vast range
of engagements with Baudrillard that can be found in circulation
now. Work on Baudrillard is as vibrant and varied as ever, with
people still using his thought as ways of approaching philosophical, technological, media, and social/cultural concerns, as well as
those related to art, science fiction, contemporary fiction, politics,
new media, visual culture, and screen culture. The chapters in this
text that extend Baudrillard's thought might prove demanding for
those not steeped in the discussions he is involved in, but, as with
Baudrillard himself, there is plenty on offer to intrigue, confound,
provoke, and provide pleasure to readers new to the topic or
currently working and writing in the field themselves.

Revisiting Baudrillard in the extensions of his work by bringing him into explicit dialogue with other thinkers (e.g. Hegel, Lingis, Foucault, Bion, and Derrida) or reading his rhetorical engagement with important and powerful discursive practices (e.g. teleologies, eschatologies, subject–object relations, the Cold War, and European conceptualizations of America through centuries of stereotypes) intend to highlight but a few ways in which returning to Baudrillard, *using* his thought, and mining his vital critical enterprise challenges thinkers in the present to work his ideas in a more thorough fashion. There has been a tendency in Baudrillard studies to adopt inadvertently his Manichean strategies (ones used for both rhetorical and conceptual effects) and thus either lapse into hagiography or outright dismissal. Those who see themselves as the keepers of "the master's" flame, just as those who wish to blow out the torch, miss the challenge that resides in, and that *is*, his writings. Little is served by drawing the circle of Baudrillard scholars closer in solipsistic utterances of mutual satisfaction and self-assured certitude just as little is gained by the blithe dismissals of Baudrillard from those who close their ears to his words by mumbling repeatedly they have heard this all before or saying that we know everything he has to say already. Both sides ultimately ignore the work.

The critical theory landscape has been profoundly changed by Baudrillard's work, and the ramifications of his writings as well as how his writings achieve their effects remain fecund terrain. The chapters included in this book are ones that generally view Baudrillard in a positive light, exploring the extensivity and intensity of his writings. Several of the contributors to the volume challenge Baudrillard. Some have in the past, and continue in the present, to openly reject some of his thought. But each finds the engagement and the challenge important and worthwhile. Baudrillard's thought has not ended, and it requires attention. And it is thought – engaged, provocative, and surprising thought – that Baudrillard most demands from us and has to offer us. The end of Baudrillard is premature. In this manner, the volume hopes to be much more than an introductory text and more than just a work aimed only at those engaged in the discussions raging around the issues that consumed Baudrillard, which are the issues of our day, of the now.

Note

1 http://www.dow.com/Hu/

References

Baudrillard, Jean (1988) *America*. Trans. Chris Turner. London: Verso.

Jean Baudrillard (1998) "In the Shadow of the Millennium, or the Suspense of the Year 2000," *C Theory* (http://www.ctheory.net/printer.aspx?id=104) published September 23, 1998, trans. Francois Debrix.

Jean Baudrillard (2001) "Photography or Light-Writing," in *Impossible Exchange*. New York: Verso.

Jean Baudrillard (2005) *The Intelligence of Evil or the Lucidity Pact*. Trans. Chris Turner. Oxford: Berg.

Jean Baudrillard and Enrique Valiente Noailles (2007) *Exiles from Dialogue*. Trans. Chris Turner. Cambridge: Polity.

1

Jean Baudrillard (1929–2007):
A Critical Overview

Douglas Kellner

On March 6, 2007 Jean Baudrillard died in Paris at the age of 77 after a long fight with cancer. Associated with postmodern and poststructuralist theory, Baudrillard is difficult to situate in relation to traditional and contemporary philosophy.[1] His work combines philosophy, social theory, and an idiosyncratic cultural metaphysics that reflects on key events of phenomena of the epoch. A sharp critic of contemporary society, culture, and thought, Baudrillard is often seen as a major guru of French postmodern theory, although he can also be read as a thinker who combines theory and social and cultural criticism in original and provocative ways and a writer who has developed his own style and forms of writing. He is an extremely prolific author who published over 50 books and commented on some of the most salient cultural and sociological phenomena of the contemporary era, including the erasure of the distinctions of gender, race, and class that structured modern societies in a new postmodern consumer, media, and high-technology society; the mutating roles of art and aesthetics; fundamental changes in politics, culture, and human beings; and the impact of new media, information, and cybernetic technologies in the creation of a qualitatively different social order, providing fundamental mutations of human and social life.

For some years a cult figure of postmodern theory, Baudrillard moved beyond the discourse of the postmodern from the early 1980s to the present, and developed a highly idiosyncratic mode of philosophical and cultural analysis that could be described as a post-poststructuralist mode of thought, although Baudrillard's theorizing is hard to categorize and pin down and often undergoes surprising mutations. Of postmodern and poststructuralist thinkers, he has consistently gone his own way and avoided fads and intellectual turns of the moment. In retrospect, he emerges from within the perspective of contemporary theory as one of the most radical post-poststructuralist thinkers who undermines key categories of Western philosophy and contemporary theory.

Baudrillard was born in the cathedral town of Reims, France, in 1929. He told interviewers that his grandparents were peasants and his parents became civil servants. He also claims that he was the first member of his family to pursue an advanced education and that this led to a rupture with his parents and cultural milieu. In 1956, he began working as a professor of secondary education in a French high school (Lyceé) and in the early 1960s did editorial work for the French publisher Seuil. Baudrillard was initially a Germanist who published essays on literature in *Les temps modernes* from 1962–3 and translated works of Peter Weiss and Bertolt Brecht into French, as well as a book on messianic revolutionary movements by Wilhelm Mühlmann. During this period, he met Henri Lefebvre, whose critiques of everyday life impressed him, and Roland Barthes, whose semiological analyses of contemporary society had lasting influence on his work.

In 1966, Baudrillard entered the University of Paris, Nanterre, and became Lefebvre's assistant, while studying languages, philosophy, sociology, and other disciplines. He defended his "These de Troisième Cycle" in sociology at Nanterre in 1966 with a dissertation on "Le système des objects," and began teaching sociology in October of that year. Opposing French and US intervention in the Algerian and Vietnamese wars, Baudrillard associated himself with the French Left in the 1960s. Nanterre was the center of radical politics and the "March 22 movement," associated with Daniel Cohn-Bendit and the *enrageés*, began in the Nanterre sociology department. Baudrillard said later that he was involved in the events of May 1968 which resulted in massive student uprisings and a general strike that almost drove French President Charles de Gaulle from power. During the late 1960s, Baudrillard began publishing a series of books that would eventually make him world famous. Influenced by Lefebvre, Barthes, Georges Bataille, and the French situationists, Baudrillard undertook serious work in the field of social theory, semiology, and psychoanalysis in the 1960s and published his first book, *The System of Objects*, in 1968 (1996), followed by *The Consumer Society* in 1970 (1998), and *For a Critique of the Political Economy of the Sign* in 1972 (1981). These early publications are attempts, within the framework of critical sociology, to combine the studies of everyday life initiated by Lefebvre and Debord and the situationists with a social semiology that studies the life of signs in social life. This project, influenced by Barthes, centers on the system of objects in the consumer society (the focus of his first two books), and the interface between political economy and semiotics (the nucleus of his third book).

Baudrillard's early work was one of the first to appropriate semiology to analyze how objects are encoded with a system of signs and meanings that constitute contemporary media and consumer societies. Combining semiological studies, Marxian political economy, and sociology of the consumer society, Baudrillard began his life-long task of exploring the system of objects and signs that forms our everyday life.

Baudrillard distanced himself from Marxism in *The Mirror of Production* (1975 [1973]) where he argues that Marxism, first, does not adequately illuminate premodern societies which were organized around symbolic exchange and not production. He also argues that Marxism does not radically enough critique capitalist societies and calls for a more extreme break. At this stage, Baudrillard turns to anthropological perspectives on premodern societies for hints of more emancipatory alternatives. Yet it is important to note that this critique of Marxism was taken from the Left, arguing that Marxism did not provide a radical enough critique of, or alternative to, contemporary productivist societies, capitalist and communist. Baudrillard concluded that French communist failure to support the May 1968 movements was rooted in part in a conservatism that had roots in Marxism itself. Hence, Baudrillard and others of his generation began searching for more radical critical positions.

His next book, *Symbolic Exchange and Death* (1993 [1976]), attempts to provide ultraradical perspectives that overcome the limitations of an economistic Marxist tradition. This ultra-leftist phase of Baudrillard's itinerary would be short-lived, however, though in *Symbolic Exchange and Death* Baudrillard produces one of his most important and dramatic provocations. In this text, Baudrillard posits a divide in history as radical as the rupture between premodern symbolic societies and modern capitalism. In the mode of classical social theory, he systematically develops distinctions between premodern societies organized around symbolic exchange, modern societies organized around production, and postmodern societies organized around simulation.

Against the organizing principles of modern and postmodern society, Baudrillard valorizes the logic of symbolic exchange, as an alternative organizing principle of society. Against modern demands to produce value and meaning, Baudrillard calls for their extermination and annihilation, providing as examples Mauss's gift exchange, Saussure's anagrams, and Freud's concept of the death drive. In all of these instances, there is a rupture with the logic of exchange (of goods, meanings, and libidinal energies) and thus an escape from the logic of production, capitalism, rationality, and meaning. Baudrillard's paradoxical logic of symbolic exchange can be explained as expression of a desire to liberate himself from modern positions and to seek a revolutionary position outside contemporary society. Against modern values, Baudrillard advocates their annihilation and extermination.

Symbolic Exchange and Death and the succeeding studies in *Simulation and Simulacra* (1994 [1981]) articulate the principle of a fundamental rupture between modern and postmodern societies and mark Baudrillard's departure from the problematic of modern social theory. For Baudrillard, modern societies are organized around the production and consumption of commodities, while postmodern societies are organized around simulation and the play of images and signs, denoting a situation in which codes, models, and signs are the organizing principles of a new social order where simulation rules. In the society of simulation, identities are constructed by the appropriation of images, and codes and models determine how individuals perceive themselves and relate to other people. Economics, politics, social life, and culture are all governed by the logic of simulation, whereby codes and models determine how goods are consumed and used, politics unfold, culture is produced and consumed, and everyday life is lived.

Baudrillard's thought from the mid-1970s to the present revolves in its own theoretical orbit and provides a set of challenging provocations to modern theory. During the 1980s, Baudrillard's major works of the 1970s were translated into many languages and each new book of the 1980s was in turn translated into English and other major languages in short order. Consequently, he became world-renowned as one of the master thinkers of postmodernity, one of the major avatars of the postmodern turn. Hence, he became something of an academic celebrity, traveling around the world promoting his work and winning a significant following, though more outside the field of academic sociology or philosophy than within any particular discipline.

At the same time that his work was becoming extremely popular, Baudrillard's own writing became increasingly difficult and occasionally hermetic. Baudrillard's new metaphysical speculations are evident in *Fatal Strategies* (1983, translated in 1990), another turning point in his itinerary. This text presented a bizarre metaphysical scenario concerning the triumph of objects over subjects within the "obscene" proliferation of an object world so completely out of control that it surpasses all attempts to understand, conceptualize, and control it. His scenario concerns the proliferation and growing supremacy of objects over subjects and the eventual triumph of the object. In a discussion of "Ecstasy and Inertia," Baudrillard discusses how objects and events in contemporary society are continually surpassing themselves, growing and expanding in power. The "ecstasy" of objects is their proliferation and expansion to the Nth degree, to the superlative; ecstasy as going outside of or beyond oneself: the beautiful as more beautiful than beautiful in fashion, the real more real than the real in television, sex more sexual than sex in pornography. Ecstasy is thus the form of obscenity (fully explicit, nothing hidden) and of the hyperreality described by Baudrillard earlier taken to a higher level, redoubled and intensified. His vision of contemporary society exhibits a careening of growth and excrescence (*croissance et excroissance*), expanding and excreting ever more goods, services, information, messages or demands – surpassing all rational ends and boundaries in a spiral of uncontrolled growth and replication.

Yet growth, acceleration, and proliferation have reached such extremes, Baudrillard suggests, that the ecstasy of excrescence is accompanied by inertia. For as the society is saturated to the limit, it implodes and winds down into entropy. This process presents a catastrophe for the subject, for not only does the acceleration and proliferation of the object world intensify the aleatory dimension of chance and non-determinacy, but also the objects themselves take over in a "cool" catastrophe for the exhausted subject, whose fascination with the play of objects turns to apathy, stupefaction, and an entropic inertia.

In retrospect, the growing power of the world of objects over the subject has been Baudrillard's theme from the beginning, thus pointing to an underlying continuity in his project. In his early writings, he explored the ways that commodities were fascinating individuals in the consumer society and the ways that the world of goods was assuming new and more value through the agency of sign value and the code – which were part of the world of things, the system of objects. His polemics against Marxism were fueled by the belief that sign value and the code were more fundamental than such traditional elements of political economy as exchange value, use value, production, and so on in constituting contemporary society. Then, reflections on the media entered the forefront of his thought: the TV object was at the center of the home in Baudrillard's earlier thinking and the media, simulations, hyperreality, and implosion eventually came to obliterate distinctions between private and public, inside and outside, media and reality. Henceforth, everything was public, transparent, ecstatic, and hyperreal in the object world, which was gaining in fascination and seductiveness as the years went by.

And so ultimately the subject, the darling of modern philosophy, is defeated in Baudrillard's metaphysical scenario and the object triumphs, a stunning end to the dialectic of subject and object that had been the framework of modern philosophy. The object is thus the subject's fatality and Baudrillard's "fatal strategies" project a paradoxical call to submit to the strategies and ruses of objects.

In *The Fatal Strategies* and succeeding writings, Baudrillard seems to be taking his unique form of theory into the realm of metaphysics, but it is a specific type of metaphysics deeply inspired by the pataphysics developed by Alfred Jarry. Like Jarry's pataphysics, Baudrillard's universe is ruled by surprise, reversal, hallucination, blasphemy, obscenity, and a desire to shock and outrage. Thus, in view of the growing supremacy of the object, Baudrillard wants us to abandon the subject and to side with the object. Pataphysics aside, it seems that Baudrillard is trying to end the philosophy of subjectivity that has controlled French thought since Descartes by going over completely to the other side. Descartes's *malin genie*, his evil genius, was a ruse of the subject that tried to seduce him into accepting what was not clear and distinct, but over which he was ultimately able to prevail. Baudrillard's "evil genius" is the object itself, which is much more malign than the merely epistemological deceptions of the subject faced by Descartes and which constitutes a fatal destiny that demands the end of the philosophy of subjectivity. Henceforth, for Baudrillard, we live in the era of the reign of the object.

Throughout his life Nietzsche was a major influence,[2] and especially in the last decades of his work, Nietzschean motifs, modes of thought, and writing practices increasingly informed his work. Baudrillard became increasingly radical and "un-contemporary," standing alone against current trends and fashions, in a fiercely individualistic mode of thought. Nietzschean categories like fate, reversal, uncertainty, and an aristocratic assault on conventional wisdom began to shape his writings, that often, à la Nietzsche, took the form of aphorisms or short essays.

In the 1980s, Baudrillard posited an "immanent reversal," a reversal of direction and meaning, in which things turn into their opposite. Thus, the society of production was passing over to simulation and seduction; the panoptic and repressive power theorized by Foucault was turning into a cynical and seductive power; the liberation championed in the 1960s was to become a form of voluntary servitude; sovereignty had passed from the side of the subject to the object; and revolution and emancipation had turned into their opposites, snaring one more and more in the logic of the system, thus trapping individuals in an order of simulation and virtuality. His concept of "immanent reversal" also provides a perverse form of Horkheimer and Adorno's *Dialectic of Enlightenment* (1972 [1947]), where everything becomes its opposite – where Enlightenment becomes domination, where culture becomes culture industry, where democracy becomes a form of mass manipulation, and science and technology part of an apparatus of domination.

Baudrillard follows this logic into the 1990s where his thought becomes ever more hermetic, metaphysical, and idiosyncratic. During this period, Baudrillard continued playing the role of academic and media superstar, traveling around the world lecturing and performing in academic and cultural events. Some of his experiences are captured in the travelogue *America* (1988) and collections of aphorisms, *Cool Memories* (1990) and *Cool Memories II* (1996), that combine reflections on his travels and experiences with development of his ideas and perceptions. Retiring from the University of Nanterre in 1987, Baudrillard subsequently functioned as an independent intellectual, dedicating himself to caustic reflections on our contemporary moment, and his metaphysical ruminations.

During the 1990s and until his death, Baudrillard continued to write short journal entries and by 2007 had published five volumes of his *Cool Memories*. He produced as well reflections on contemporary issues like the Gulf War, the September 11 terror attacks, which he saw as the only real "event" of the past decades, globalization, the US invasion of Iraq, and other occurrences of the day.[3] Baudrillard also continued his metaphysical speculations in works such as *The Transparency of Evil* (1993 [1990]), *The Illusion of the End* (1994b [1992]), *The Perfect Crime* (1996b [1995]), *Impossible Exchange* (2001 [1999], *The Intelligence of Evil or the Lucidity Pact* (2005), and *The Conspiracy of Art* (2005).

Baudrillard has never been as influential in France as in the English-speaking world and elsewhere – a point made in many French obituaries and blogs upon his death. Baudrillard is an example of the "global popular," a thinker who has followers and readers throughout the world, though, so far, no Baudrillardian school has emerged.[4] His influence has been largely at the margins of a diverse number of disciplines ranging from social theory to philosophy to art history, thus it is difficult to gauge his impact on the mainstream of philosophy, or any specific academic discipline. Baudrillard is perhaps most important as part of the postmodern turn against modernity and its academic disciplines. Baudrillard's work cuts across the disciplines and promotes cross-disciplinary thought. He challenges standard wisdom and puts in question received dogma and methods. While his early work on the consumer society, the political economy of the sign, simulation and simulacra, and the implosion of phenomena previously separated can be deployed within critical theory, much of his post-1980s work quite self-consciously goes beyond the classical tradition.

Baudrillard thus emerges as a transdisciplinary theorist of the fin-de-millennium, a critical radical of modernity and modern theory, and a harbinger of an emergent (post-)postmodern mode of thought and discourse. In the final analysis, Baudrillard is perhaps most useful as a provocateur who challenges and puts in question the tradition of classical social theory and philosophy, and standard academic disciplines and procedures. He claims that the object of classical theory – modernity – has been surpassed by a novel social situation, called "postmodernity" by some, and that therefore new theoretical strategies, modes of writing, and forms of theory are necessary.

Baudrillard thus ultimately goes beyond conventional sociology and theory altogether into his own theoretical sphere and mode of writing that provides occasionally biting insights into contemporary social phenomena and provocative critiques of contemporary and classical thought. He now appears in retrospect as a completely idiosyncratic thinker who went his own way and developed his own mode of writing and thought. Baudrillard had a good, long run, and we will miss his acerbic irony, provocations, and challenges to contemporary thought and discourse.

Notes

1 For a fuller explication of Baudrillard's relation to philosophy see my entry on Baudrillard in the *Stanford Encyclopedia of Philosophy* at

http://plato.stanford.edu/entries/baudrillard/, and the more extended version published as "Jean Baudrillard After Modernity: Provocations On A Provocateur and Challenger," *International Journal of Baudrillard Studies*, 3, 1, January 2006, at http://www.ubishops.ca/baudrillardstudies/vol3_1/kellner.htm. For the first book published on Baudrillard and an overview of early stages of his work, see Douglas Kellner, *Jean Baudrillard: From Marxism to Post-Modernism and Beyond*, Cambridge, UK and Palo Alto, CA: Polity Press and Stanford University Press, 1989.

2 See Arthur Kroker, "The Spirit of Jean Baudrillard: In Memoriam: 1929–2007," *C-Theory* (posted March 8, 2007) at http://www.ctheory.net/articles.aspx?id=573.htm.

3 On this work, see my "Baudrillard, Globalization and Terrorism: Some Comments on Recent Adventures of the Image and Spectacle on the Occasion of Baudrillard's 75th Birthday," *International Journal of Baudrillard Studies*, 2, 1, January 2005) at http://www.ubishops.ca/baudrillardstudies/vol2_1/kellner.htm.

4 There is, however, an excellent Internet journal edited by Gerry Coulter, *International Journal of Baudrillard Studies* at http://www.ubishops.ca/baudrillardstudies/index.html.

Major theoretical works by Jean Baudrillard

(1996c [1968]) *The System of Objects*. London: Verso.

(1998 [1970]) *The Consumer Society*. London: Verso.

(1975 [1973]) *The Mirror of Production*. St. Louis, MO: Telos Press.

(1981 [1973]) *For a Critique of the Political Economy of the Sign*. St. Louis, MO: Telos Press.

(1983a) *Simulations*. New York: Semiotext(e).

(1983b) *In the Shadow of the Silent Majorities*. New York: Semiotext(e).

(1983c) "The Ecstacy of Communication," in *The Anti-Aesthetic*, ed. Hal Foster. Port Townsend, WA: Bay Press.

(1988) *America*. London: Verso.

(1990a) *Cool Memories*. London: Verso.

(1990b) *Fatal Strategies*. New York: Semiotext(e).

(1993a) *Symbolic Exchange and Death*. London: Sage.

(1993b) *The Transparency of Evil*. London: Verso.

(1994a) *Simulacra and Simulation*. Ann Arbor, MI: University of Michigan Press.

(1994b) *The Illusion of the End*. Oxford: Polity Press.

(1995) *The Gulf War Never Happened*. Oxford: Polity Press.

(1996a) *Cool Memories II*. Oxford: Polity Press.

(1996b) *The Perfect Crime*. London and New York: Verso Books.

(1997) *Fragments: Cool Memories III, 1990–1995*. London and New York: Verso Books.

(2000) *The Vital Illusion*. New York: Columbia University Press.

(2001) *Impossible Exchange*. London: Verso.

(2002a) *The Spirit of Terrorism: And Requiem for the Twin Towers*. London: Verso.

(2002b) *Screened Out*. London: Verso.

(2005a) *The Intelligence of Evil or the Lucidity Pact*. Trans. Chris Turner. Oxford: Berg.

(2005b) *The Conspiracy of Art*. New York: Semiotext(e).

2

Baudrillard and the Evil Genius

Ryan Bishop and John Phillips

Thought must play a catastrophic role, must be itself an element of
catastrophe, of provocation in a world that wants absolutely to cleanse
everything, to exterminate death and negativity. But it must at the
same time remain humanist, concerned for the human, and, to that
end, recapture the reversibility of good and evil, of the human and the
inhuman.

Jean Baudrillard, *Passwords*, 92

To approach the legacy of Jean Baudrillard is to engage on three
levels, in registers that can only in theory be separated, for in fact
they operate together as if within the dramatic efficacy of a single
gesture. Baudrillard appears first of all as a prophet of apocalypse.
The world has become dominated by systems that signify, in all
their objects and events, the abstractions that serve the idea of
their rapid expansion: speed, technology, efficiency, autonomy.
Everything that serves a function becomes, in a world where everything must increasingly serve a function, a sign of the abstraction
functionality.

But Baudrillard is also the analyst, the semiologist, and the critic
of these systems, of the identifications they impose and of the
imaginary *truths* they create. Technical innovations that connote

increased autonomy are nonetheless dysfunctional in introducing further complexity and increased dependence upon the heterogeneity of systems. One simple example from the many produced in *The System of Objects* [*Les système des objets*, 1968] illustrates the point: "From the strictly technological standpoint, the elimination of the starting-handle makes the mechanical operation of cars more complicated, because it subordinates it to the use of electrical power from a storage battery that is external to the system" (117). So a technical innovation can *connote* technical autonomy while actually reducing it, rendering obsolete the actually more autonomous system that has been replaced and is now experienced as a nostalgic throwback to a primitive past.

From *The System of Objects* (1968) to *The Intelligence of Evil* (2005) Baudrillard discovers systems operating according to the unending, because technically impossible, imperative to integrate the heterogeneous on the imaginary level of connotation, while simultaneously multiplying heterogeneity. The realm of imaginary truths created by the abstraction of systems, and analyzed painstakingly in *The System of Objects*, bears a perverse, disconnected relation to the *real*. The *real*, which has hitherto been dominated by the bourgeois system of social relations, of individuals, objects, and exchange, is with increasing intensity replaced by systems of abstraction driven by the idea of functionality. *Functionality* is itself the abstraction of *function*; an object does not *actually* need to function for it to signify functionality (as the example of tail fins on cars demonstrates). So a new vocabulary is required by which one can explore the effects of abstraction, and its systems of imaginary truth, on the institutions and social ensembles that actually live by them.

The logic of simulacra and the hyperreal involves an increased reliance on systems of functionality that bear no relation to any real other than that connoted by them (this is the so-called *hyperreal*). The fact that these systems are fundamentally concerned with the *production of meaning* and the *reduction of meaning to information* does not lessen their impact on the heterogeneous activities of mortals in the world: the interaction of media, policing, surveillance technologies, computer technologies, military operations, genetic, biological, and molecular control all serve to *render apparent*, as

Baudrillard establishes, for instance, in his analysis of *obscenity* in *The Ecstasy of Communication* (the original version published as *L'Autre par lui-même* in 1987). An intensification of the drive to render all objects and events totally apparent and absolutely integrated inevitably produces an intensification of the barriers against this drive, and this symbiotic antagonism comes to represent for Baudrillard – in the guise of what he begins from the mid-1980s to call "the great game" – the greatest challenge for contemporary social thought.

One drive involves a "project" that aims to render everything *real* in the abstract sense, according to which everything becomes transparent. This is what, in *The Intelligence of Evil*, Baudrillard calls "Integral Reality." The dominant modes of Integral Reality are those of the media (broadcasting, TV, computers), which display everything (rather than certain things). Baudrillard is particularly concerned to identify the symptomatic display of what is rendered *needlessly* visible, an increasingly redundant transparency of banal images that in *The Ecstasy of Communication* he describes as *obscene*. The most immediate examples are the so-called Reality TV programs, "where everything is put on view and you realize there no longer is anything to see" (*Intelligence of Evil*, 93). These symptomatically banal images come about as the result of a project that aims to eradicate all forms of secrecy, of seduction, of surprise, and thus of anything that would amount to an *event*.

Against this "relentless banality" but at the same time from within it, as its inevitable reversal, emerges the "intelligence of evil," or the "dual drive," which is grounded on everything that resists the project of "integral reality," everything that resists transparency and the reality principle. So in effect the game describes the putting into play of a drive that militates constantly against anything that fails to appear as such and against anything that might happen (this is what *evil* means today). In the mode of analysis established already by *The System of Objects*, Baudrillard identifies the drive as hostile to anything that threatens to fall outside the abstraction into which the real has, as he puts it, "disappeared." Tele-media reporters, for instance, tend to arrive at scenes of catastrophe first, before emergency services, so that the coding of reportage seems always already "there," in advance of any event, which in these ways is prevented from *happening*. The power characteristic of the integral drive is based, in Baudrillard's argument, entirely on "the prevention and policing of events" (*Intelligence of Evil*, 121). A typically striking and notorious political example would be the war in Iraq, whose aim was supposedly the *prevention* in advance of Saddam's use of weapons of mass destruction. Prevention, of course, can also work retrospectively, as the operations in Afghanistan demonstrate: a seemingly endless mitigation for the attacks on the Twin Towers.

Baudrillard's analyses identify, first, the "insignificance" of traditional forms of political resistance and, second, the kind of power that might actually be effective against the "*Realpolitik*" of contemporary operations like the war in Iraq: their own internal limitations. "If the worldwide demonstrations against war may have produced the illusion of a possible counter-power," he argues, "they demonstrated above all the political insignificance of this 'international community' by comparison with American *Realpolitik*" (*Intelligence of Evil*, 120). But the power of Integral Reality is brought to bear "against itself, by all kinds of internal failures" (121). An internal failure would manifest where a "troubling strangeness" by chance erupts to disturb the banality of "the global order." And because this can happen at any time the global order is set up with increasing intensity to militate against such chances, against chance itself, against the "luck of the event," as Baudrillard puts it, suggesting that perhaps that is all we have left.

In a dark twist, those who spring to the defense of what they call the real, mistaking Baudrillard's analyses for the attack itself, risk replicating the murder of the real by "Integral Reality." To question the representations that pass themselves off as reality is not to attack the real itself; yet it is this questioning that Baudrillard's critics often castigate him for. His responses mildly parody the absurdity of such criticism: "any questioning of reality, of its obviousness and its principle, is deemed unacceptable and condemned as negationist" (*Intelligence of Evil*, 22). Writing in response to numerous such objections, he continues "if you speak of the simulacrum, then you are a simulator; if you speak of the virtuality of war, then you are in league with it and have no regard for the hundreds of thousands of dead" (23). The simplistic conflation of message and messenger,

Baudrillard suggests, aligns itself unwittingly with the constitution of the integral power it seeks to resist, for residing within Integral Reality and necessary for its realization is its own resistance, which it ceaselessly generates as an unavoidable function of its immanent structure.

The increasingly disabling deadlock of this great game brings us to the third register of Baudrillard's modes of participation: that of the devising and implementation of strategies. It is imperative, under conditions that Baudrillard sets out, to avoid the patterns that describe the incessant give and take of the drive for integration and the drive that reciprocally – as a function of the same force – opposes it. The diversity of strategic intervention that marks the development of Baudrillard's career – for instance, the devising of "four phases of the image" and "three orders of simulacra" – replicates a logic of replacement that cleverly disguises a concern for what remains most consistent in Baudrillard's mode of presentation, but which could not have survived in the familiar and recognizable form of a name. As is well-known, "the successive phases of the image" schematized in *Simulacra and Simulation* [*Simulacres et simulation*, 1981] chart a continuous movement through four phases from *representation*, as faithful "reflection of a profound reality," to *simulation*, which "has no relation to any reality whatsoever" (*Simulacra and Simulation*, 6). What consistently marks each of the phases leading up to the fourth is a level of secrecy, of something hidden, of something being missing or absent from the field of representation. A reality is "reflected" or "denatured," or its "absence" is "masked," but it is never actually *present*. Only in the fourth phase is everything present and transparent. Baudrillard's strategies, then, involve interventions that aim to evoke, alongside these analyses (of abstraction, the system of objects, the world as simulacrum, etc.), fields of silence, of seduction, and of evil. In different ways what disappears can somehow be mobilized without it being made to appear as such.

Intellectual histories, or biographies, of Baudrillard's career tend to see his work in narrative stages – typically: the emergence from Marxism and the "mode of production," to the paradigmatic form of a post-Marxism and the "mode of information," via the semiotic medium of the sign. Such histories inevitably fail to do justice to the consistency of a strategic response, which patient and responsive reading can reveal. We should probably acknowledge the resources of an intellectual heritage that were often silently mobilized in his work or alluded to subtly, without fanfare: the hyperbolic invention of the malicious demon (*genium malignum*) from the first of Descartes's *Meditations* (see *Ecstasy of Communication*, 75); Marcel Duchamp's invention from *nothing* of possibly the most widely recognized artwork of the twentieth century (*Fountain* by R. Mutt); or Lichtenberg's enigmatic aphorism about the "knife with no blade and no handle," subverted with affirmation in critical essays that no one could get a handle on or see what their points were. The notorious "Lichtenberg Knife" is productive for evoking its object through a periphrasis on "nothing" (the description of the knife is of course a roundabout way of saying "nothing" – Sigmund Freud refers to it in connection with Carl Jung's schismatic appropriation of psychoanalysis). Baudrillard evokes it (for apparently the first time) in one of his eleven aphoristic theses from 1971, "L'utopie a été renvoyée" [*Utopia Deferred*]: "Utopia, through the abolition of the blade and the disappearance of the handle, gives the knife its power to strike" (*Utopia Deferred*, 62). The periphrasis allows the knife to linger a while before it disappears entirely so that the trace of its disappearance does not disappear. The subtlety of a strategy that mobilizes *nothing* as an effective methodological principle emerges in the early 1970s, in association with a group of interdisciplinary intellectuals involved in the journal *Utopie*.

From there he develops an idiom of analysis at a tangent to mainstream disciplinary formations, one that operates at the axes of social theory, political economy, semiotics, psychoanalysis, media analysis, art, architecture, urbanism, and literature. Throughout he remains at arm's length from intellectual movements, schools, and cliques, despite his reputation for being otherwise. Baudrillard's idiom is singular and unmistakable yet it incorporates a variety of styles. His writing tends to build on an aphoristic way with the sentence and can move quickly from prophetic and analytic statements to classical (humanist) techniques from the ancient arts of persuasion; but sentences can also gather into sustained and painstaking analyses. The sententiousness, in its pithy hyperbole, serves to subvert *the sentence itself* in a fatalism that he attributes

.e world is fatal, let us be more fatal than it. If
.et us be more indifferent. We must conquer the
.ce it through an indifference that is at least equal to
(*Ecstasy of Communication*, 101). This pithy hyperbole
it is so seductive in its own way and therefore courts
ı.   ı – perhaps overshadows the subtlety and consistency of
his arguments.

The point is that, whatever system is under analysis – which in
Baudrillard's acute gaze is always a sign of what is to come, the
most aggressive or most rapidly emergent tendencies of the time
– it is what most subtly eludes or evades it, what it least can accom-
modate to itself, that helps to mobilize Baudrillard's response to it.
In *The Intelligence of Evil* he is quite plain about it. A "collective
choice" follows a line of flight "into the abstraction of the virtual,"
which "absolves us of any personal responsibility" (*Intelligence of
Evil*, 90). This notion of "personal responsibility" is nonetheless quite difficult, because for it to have any purchase it must be
withdrawn from the abstraction of the *real* (there is no functional
difference in this book between notions of real and hyperreal) and
somehow rediscovered as the irreducible strangeness of momentary
experience. The role of the "personal" is revealed as that which is
most threatened: "an image," he argues, "affects us directly, below
the level of representation: at the level of intuition, of perception.
At that level, the image is always an absolute surprise. At least
it should be" (91). The problem with images is that they have
suffered a "fall into the real":

> We commonly say that the real has disappeared beneath a welter of
> signs and images, and it is true that there is a violence of the image. But
> that violence is substantially offset by the violence done to the image:
> its exploitation for documentary purposes, as testimony or message,
> its exploitation for moral, political or promotional ends, or simply for
> purposes of information. . ." (*Intelligence of Evil*, 91–2)

The subtle reversal of what perhaps is familiar from lazy commen-
taries on Baudrillard's supposed claim regarding the "loss of the
real" ("we commonly say") finds not the real suffering under the
image but the image suffering a fall into the real.

Baudrillard's reference to personal responsibility indicates, of course, his consistent concern: whether the real suffers or the image suffers, the procedure is always at the cost of a responsibility reduced by systems of abstraction. Elements of representation, whether images, signs, or metaphors, will not register on a personal, intuitive, perceptive level, so long as they are allowed to circulate as merely the vehicles of meaning, events of communication, or the media of information – as disposable means for an end. This is what is meant by personal responsibility: the ability (which might also be the will) to invest a sign with an alien property that is estranged from both the individual – the "subject" addressed by it – and *the person* who thus becomes surprised by it and responsible for it. The analysis of advertising in *The System of Objects* had been mobilized already by this singular concern. "It is not," he argues there, "that advertising 'alienates' or 'mystifies' us with its claims, words or images; rather we are swayed by the fact that 'they' are sufficiently concerned to want to address us, to show us things, to take an interest in us" (*System of Objects*, 185). This mode of address fulfills a tendency to abstraction that maintains the passage from function to functionality: advertising functions not simply on the model of personal relationship (the bourgeois individual and his objects in exchange) but as an abstraction – a simulation – of personal relationship, in which the addressee is *produced* by the mode of address.

The ways in which an individual can be "swayed" militate each time against anything that reserves itself from the process. When Baudrillard introduces the registers of *seduction* into his analyses it seems to be as a way of reserving from the glare of the visible (following Paul Virilio's "aesthetics of disappearance") an element of secrecy, mystery, an element of the alien. Advertising, in the earlier analysis, precisely does not mystify or seduce its addressee. In the more recent analyses, in which "integral visibility" unites "the banality of the image" with "the banality of life" so that there "no longer is anything to see" (*Intelligence of Evil*, 93), brings to a higher level of intensity the observations made in *The Ecstasy of Communication*, according to which: "the fury to unveil the truth, to get at the naked truth, the one which haunts all discourses of interpretation, the obscene rage to uncover the secret, is proportionate to the impossibility of ever achieving this" (*Ecstasy of Communication*, 73). So it might seem that if Baudrillard opposes a discourse of the secret to abstract discourses of interpretation, information, truth, and representation, then this discourse will take the form of a kind of opacity of the image or the sign (the signifier as opposed to the abstract signified). But this could not be more wrong. The opposition of visibility and opacity simply confirms and replicates the pattern of the great game. Somewhere between the ideality of signified meaning (the first order of simulacra) and the productive mode of the signifier (the second order) lies an indeterminate and strictly invisible and silent critical gap – the space of personal responsibility itself. This is what in the early 1970s is designated by "Utopia," which in the sixth thesis on "Utopia Deferred . . ." is "the gap, the fault, the void that passes between the signifier and the signified and subverts every sign" (*Utopia Deferred*, 62). In the brief article "Simulacra and Science Fiction," this space of critical responsibility, as a kind of gap or distance between orders that allows for a "critical projection," is permanently threatened by the closure of the third order of simulacra: "from one order of simulacra to another, the tendency is certainly towards the reabsorption of this distance, of this gap that leaves room for an ideal or critical projection" (*Simulacra and Simulation*, 121–2).

The impossible and the nonexistent have no place in the order of precession of simulacra. But in Baudrillard's analyses it is exactly the domain of the impossible, of what disappears and thus remains seductive, that is reserved, and which thus leaves open the consistently applied possibility of critical engagement. All of this also leaves the question of the critical response to Baudrillard open to analysis. Arguably Baudrillard is at his most prophetic, most analytic, and most strategically effective in his response to the wars of the second half of the twentieth century, yet it is on this that criticism of Baudrillard begins to lose its grip. The observation, in *Simulacra and Simulation*, that the war in Vietnam resembles in all its dimensions a test site for arms and methods of engagement, a hypothetically driven experiment designed to discover the consequences and effects of diverse innovative strategies, raises the stakes of the functionality hypothesis. In a truly ingenious strategy, Baudrillard's analysis of the war in Vietnam (a brief yet devastating application of ideas developed in the essay "The Precession of Simulacra") is made in the context of a reading of Coppola's *Apocalypse Now*. It is worth quoting a passage at length:

> Coppola makes his film the way the Americans made war . . . The war as entrenchment, as technological and psychedelic fantasy, the war as a succession of special effects, the war become film even before being filmed. The war abolishes itself in its technological test, and for Americans it was primarily that: a test site, a gigantic territory in which to test their arms, their methods, their power.
>
> Coppola does nothing but that: test cinema's *power of intervention*, test the impact of cinema that has become an immeasurable machinery of special effects. In this sense, his film is really the extension of the war through other means . . . The war became film, the film becomes war, the two are joined by their common hemorrhage into technology . . . One has understood nothing, neither about the war nor about cinema (at least the latter) if one has not grasped this lack of distinction that is no longer either an ideological or a moral one, one of good and evil, but one of the reversibility of both production and destruction, of the immanence of a thing in its very revolution, of the organic metabolism of all the technologies, of the carpet of bombs in the strip of the film . . . (*Simulacra and Simulation*, 59–60)

To state the obvious, Baudrillard's thought and writings have been the subject of much controversy. To further state the obvious, all strong readings of a given author are misreadings, as Harold Bloom suggests, but not all misreadings are strong readings. As a stylist and rhetorician of formidable power, Baudrillard often attracts such readings. As a philosophical provocateur, he has often courted controversy, and found it – no mean feat in an age of media and publishing overload. Because of his eminently quotable style, his compelling rhetoric and his willingness to flirt with hyperbole for rhetorical ends, Baudrillard is often dipped into, read far too casually, and quoted in outlandish decontextualization. His works on the United States, *America* and the *Cool Memories* series, launched a score of heated responses, both highly favorable and not. His publications after the attacks on 9/11 led to a predictable set of anti-French rants from the political right in the US and elsewhere, accusing him of condoning and celebrating terrorism. But it is not that sort of bleeding over into the public discursive sphere of pundits that is troubling; rather it is the strong misreadings of his work from within the humanities and social sciences that cause one pause. Richard Wolin's vitriolic response in *The Seduction of Unreason* (2004) is but one case in point, and there are many such cases.

As occasional harbinger of postmodernism during a moment when such post-positionings could cause consternation from various staid perspectives within disciplines, Baudrillard became the reluctant poster child for the movement. Many Marxist critics believed Baudrillard's apparent if clearly ambivalent shift from modernity to postmodernity to be an inexcusable relinquishing of a political agenda, when in fact his work shifted foci to engage the different forms of politics performed in an age of increased simulation, IT, seduction, obscenity, value crises, rampant "promiscuity of signs and values," and global pillaging. His Marxist interests and past never left his analyses, though he remained clearly ambivalent about traditional Marxist tenets, metamorphosing into a set of relations about the object and its fundamental transformations through hyperglobal capital and an increasingly "impossible exchange" characterized by an oxymoronical virtual reality no longer capable of opposing a real or of possibly being destined to actualization itself. He engaged the intensification of those processes that "screened out" the masses from participatory politics, as well as the effects they rendered on traditional bases for claims made in the name of the social.

Clearly his interests remained political, but the political has for some decades now sustained itself in intensely immaterial ways. That is, through the ceaseless project of simulation or experimentation intended to produce a regime of the real (itself not opposed to the virtual) and the good, we have been placed in the untenable position of the impossibility of resistance. To resist this project would be both capitulating to it, via the logic that it creates its own resistance, which is necessary to its operation, and opposing the real and the good. It is on those grounds – that of the immaterial but also simultaneously of the object – that his political engagements were waged. Standing at an oblique angle to conventional politics, a politics badly unraveled by the events of 1968, Baudrillard sought to explore the means by which the social and the political had been rendered immaterial, how the populace at large might be shaped by the implosion of the social into media, and provide catalysts for reconstituting political discourse and action in light of these effects.

Perhaps no other textual event or proclamation of his has inspired more misunderstanding than his work about the Gulf War, our first fully televised "real-time" conflict, in which he claimed infamously before the advent of military activity that the war would not and could not take place. He questioned its occurrence while it raged on TV screens, packaged by networks with their own theme music, slogans, titles, graphics, and even sponsors. Then once there had been a cessation of hostilities, he asserted that it had not taken place. Emblematic of the sort of responses his essays on this military phenonenon inspire is the reading provided by Christopher Norris in his book *Uncritical Theory: Postmodernsim, Intellectuals and the Gulf War,* in which he claimed that Baudrillard's editorial interventions "amounted to a grand exposure of postmodernist thinking from the inside" (Norris, 1992: 22). He responds to the later Baudrillard article, "The Gulf War Has Not Taken Place," by claiming that "one could scarcely wish for a clearer statement of the moral and political nihilism that follows from Baudrillard's far-out skeptical stance on matters of truth and falsehood" than the claims made in this brief essay (194). Norris's objections to and arguments against Baudrillard's provocative analyses are worth pausing over briefly, for Norris invokes metonymically a host of outraged responses by otherwise level-headed academicians. Norris, taking a laudably oblique tack, offers a case for separating Derrida from the more general postmodernist mess, which would include (for him) Baudrillard as well as Lyotard, Rorty, Hayden White, and Foucault, and correctly claims that authors such as Searle and Habermas have dismissed Derrida's work based on a relatively uninformed engagement with his rigorous readings of philosophical and literary texts.

Norris exhibits acumen in his arguments about Derrida's assailants and their overall straw-mannish tenor, this despite his own somewhat questionable readings of Derrida. Yet when he takes up Baudrillard directly, he falls prey to the same charge he has just leveled against Searle, Habermas, and others: quite simply, he seems not to have read Baudrillard's works well or deeply. Instead he is keen to use Baudrillard's brief editorial pieces around and about the Gulf War as symptomatic of "a cultural malaise" known as postmodernism. If Norris wishes to tick off, and he does, literary theorists and humanities scholars (many of whom promote Baudrillard) for failing to engage Derrida in a serious, critical manner because it would mean taking up the kind of "critical reading" he claims is "allied to a knowledge of developments outside the charmed circle of post-structuralist debate" (Norris, 1992: 20) then he can do so with some warranted success. However, in so doing, he leaves himself open to the same charges of superficial reading (or willed misreading), especially when he claims that Baudrillard's main predictions and points can be overturned easily by simply stating that "Baudrillard's predictions were flat wrong, that the Gulf War *did* break out as a matter of all too definite fact" (14) – a retort tantamount to the most naive of empirical counters, a petulant Johnsonian "I refute it thus" (an allusion Norris actually invokes). Clearly such claims miss the nuances and complexity of Baudrillard's arguments. That these arguments have continued to possess an ever-increasing power and sustained usefulness the further we move away from the conflict that inspired this specific manifestation of them (e.g. in relation to Waco, Somalia, Yugoslavia, Rwanda, 9/11, the War on Terror, the Iraq War, saber-rattling against Iran, and so on) reveals an abbreviated engagement with the consistency in the trajectories of Baudrillard's work and its trenchant power. More to the point, though, assertions of the supposedly irrefutable facticity of events as evidence of the failure of Baudrillard's arguments provide exquisite exemplification of the very simplistic rote modes of thought that Baudrillard wishes to combat. These polemics become a simulation of academic exchange and debate – a point exceptionally clear some fifteen years removed from the mock engagements surrounding the Gulf War writings.

The political ramifications of simulation within the symbolic and the imposition of the real through the virtual constitute the stakes of the Gulf War as Baudrillard addresses it. In so doing, he returns to analyses of terrorism and hostage-taking in the mid-1970s, incorporated into *Symbolic Exchange and Death*, that would remain in play throughout his career, and receive intensified examination, due to intensified conditions, in his 2004 *The Intelligence of Evil*. In essence, Baudrillard argues that the standard modes of resistance to political actions such as the Gulf War or the Iraq War offered by activists and intellectuals playing by outmoded rules of political engagement will not only prove ineffectual in derailing the system of simulation, but will only be a simulation of resistance itself and therefore enable the further construction of the Real operative in the simulation of politics. "It is impossible to destroy the system by a contradiction-based logic or by reversing the balance of forces – in short, by a direct, dialectical revolution affecting the economic or political infrastructure" he writes. "Everything that produces contradiction or a balance of forces or energy in general merely feeds back into the system and drives it on" (quoted in Turner, 2005: 4).

Such direct-action confrontation is exactly what many on the Left endorse, while claiming Baudrillard's position is not only nihilistic but also constitutive of an ideological complicity between strains of anti-rationalist thought and the crisis, if not actual failure, of moral and political will extant in US-EU democracies. For those still in thrall to proactive political action (and to a limited extent, who isn't?), these objections carry conviction and sway. For those who witnessed the massive demonstrations in the build-up to the Iraq War – demonstrations that included millions of participants worldwide exercising both non-violent and violent action – being summarily dismissed out of hand by "The Coalition of the Willing" as simply exercising their right to protest (a right, they hastened to remind others, not allowed in Saddam's Iraq), it is difficult not to see the UN and the protests as part of the simulation of participatory politics. "We have total information, but it has no effect," Baudrillard writes in the mid-1980s. "Information plays the role of a scalpel, forever separating the juntas in power in all the countries of the world from any collective will, and cicatrizing, as if with hot irons, the contradictions which may ensue" (*Screened Out*, 82).

Baudrillard's logic in these instances is replicated in a number of positions he takes throughout his career, including the necessity to refrain from calling Watergate a scandal, for doing so merely

proves that scandals can exist within the current regime therefore
justifying its power through its capacity for self-correction and
approval. The Gulf War essays show how the fully mediated simulacral conflict of the early 1990s fits the larger pattern of Cold War
deterrence as another means of waging conflict and thus realizing
as completely as possible the control of images and information
(disinformation). On the geopolitical scale, then, the purpose of
wars is to rein in recalcitrant regimes while sending messages to
other potential foes about the technological, military, and simulational power of the US: "the large footprint" in the sand that
the Pentagon invoked during the early period of the Iraq War – a
footprint growing fainter and smaller as the Occupation continues.
Sending a message has long been a strategy of sovereignty. About
the Gulf War, Baudrillard writes:

> Our wars have less to do with the confrontation of warriors than with
> the domestication of the refractory forces on the planet, those uncon-
> trollable elements as the police would say, to which belong not only
> Islam in its entirety but wild ethnic groups, minority languages etc. All
> that is singular and irreducible must be reduced and absorbed. This is
> the law of democracy and the New World Order. (*Gulf War*, 86)

This is, of course, too the law of the real and the good, of the
project of simulation.

   What holds true internationally for Integral Reality is even more
apparent intranationally with regard to resistance. Continuing a
point repeatedly asserted in the Gulf War essays, which has been
misunderstood or ignored by critics, Baudrillard suggests we dis-
regard the desire and impulse for direct confrontation through a
strategy of becoming "more virtual than the events themselves"
(*Gulf War*, 14). In other but directly related terms, we are to avoid
vanishing into the old arguments between the first and second
orders of simulation. In an essay entitled "The Masses" he argues
that silence in the face of the ever-unidirectional nature of media
and politics (both terms not really applicable because they presume
exchange) represents a new and "original strategy" (Poster, 1988:
208), one that allows "the individual or the mass reply by a *parodic*
behavior of disappearance" (213).

The impossible exchange (to quote another book title, one he used to characterize détente in the 1970s) that has constituted politics and media since the 1980s leaves us all very few options, and so Baudrillard reads in the silence of the masses not a complacent acquiescence to the status quo, but a continuation of the logic of reversal that hands back the gift of participatory politics along with and through electronic communications. If politics and media render us as objects that have disappeared through our engagement with them, then we can disappear of our own accord knowing how the forces at play have rendered our position thus. What are the choices left us? "We have, then, to come to terms with a contradictory situation in that we both have the system we deserve and – and equally non-negligibly – we cannot bear it," Baudrillard argues. "This is a form of insoluble dilemma. You can have a visceral anti-mass, anti-yob, anti-redneck reaction. But an equally visceral anti-elite, anti-caste, anti-culture, anti-*nomeklatura* reaction. Should you be on the side of the mindless masses or of arrogant privilege (arrogant particularly in claiming an affinity with the masses)? There is no solution" (*Screened Out*, 83).

Such a logic consistently runs throughout Baudrillard's work, a sustained logic to "be meteorologically sensitive to stupidity" (*Gulf War*, 67) and to read all events, whether deserving of the term or not, with all critical faculties engaged in ways not on the terms that have held in the past, for to do so is to participate in the great game. This does not mean, as many have suggested, a jettisoning of these terms and rules, for they are mobilized continuously and ubiquitously, but to maintain an awareness of how they now have no purchase beyond the simulacral perpetuation of Integral Reality. This perpetuation reveals an intensification over time that has increasingly codified trends in communications, technology, politics, the social, the psychological, and economics. As Baudrillard sums up in *The Ecstasy of Communication*, his presentation for the Sorbonne:

> The decisive mutations of objects and of the environment in the modern era have come from an irreversible tendency towards three things: an ever-greater formal and operational abstraction of elements and functions and their homogenization in a single virtual process of

functionalization; the displacement of bodily movements and efforts into electric or electronic commands, and the miniaturization, in time and space, of processes whose real scene (though it is no longer a scene) is that of infinitesimal memory and the screen with which they are equipped. (Foster, 1983: 128–9)

With his death in 2007, Baudrillard, born in 1929, might well be amongst the last of a formidable generation of French thinkers, including Virilio (1932), Irigaray (1930), Derrida (1930), Bourdieu (1930), Foucault (1927), Deleuze (1925), and perhaps even back to Althusser (1918) and Barthes (1915). Hailing from Reims, he claimed that his grandparents were peasants and his father a minor civil servant (with some speculation that he might have been a policeman). Initially a student of German literature and philosophy, he wrote about and translated Brecht, Peter Weiss, and others. Gradually shifting from literature (which he never truly left) to sociology under the tutelage of Lefebvre, he enrolled in the University of Paris, Nanterre, in 1966, served as Lefebvre's assistant and working with Barthes. In addition to these two, some other intellectual touchstones for Baudrillard include Jarry's pataphysics, Bataille's *The Accursed Share*, Artaud's *The Theater of Cruelty*, Mauss's *The Gift*, and, of course, Nietzsche (a mainstay from his German literature and philosophy days). In the center of the storm that became "the March 22 movement" and resulted in the well-known events of May 1968, like many of this generation, Baudrillard was deeply involved in and affected by the successes and failures of political action.

Baudrillard catapulted to fame (or, divisive as always, infamy) in the English-speaking world in the 1980s, especially with his work on simulation and simulacra, fatal strategies, and symbolic exchange, as well as his proclamation of the end of the social argued in the 1983 translation of *In the Shadow of the Silent Majorities*. As a result of this sudden fame, his works began to appear more or less simultaneously in English and French, but many of the early works remained unavailable in translation until the 1990s. The problems of sequencing due to translation delays have contributed to the complications of Baudrillard's reception in English-speaking academia, making the sustained set of trajectories apparent largely in retrospect rather than as they unfolded. Because Baudrillard was an academic "star" and a reluctant guru for the art world, a role he forcefully repudiated with *The Conspiracy of Art*, many academicians dismissed him out of hand, read him too lightly, or took him too literally – which was a trick he banked on to further prove his larger points. For all of Baudrillard's purported rhetorical flourishes and obscurantist tendencies, his capacity for rendering the complexity and interdependency of objects, commodities and events in provocative, seductive, and memorable ways continued to return over forty years. For one often accused of riding the waves of fashionable theoretical posing, Baudrillard emerges with an intellectual honesty difficult to undermine or ignore.

Selected major works by Jean Baudrillard

(2006 [1967–1978]) *Utopia Deferred: Writings for Utopie (1967–1978)*, Trans. Stuart Kendall. New York: Semiotext(e).

(1996) *The System of Objects*. Trans. James Benedict. London: Verso.

(1998 [1970]) *The Consumer Society*. Trans. Chris Turner. London: Sage.

(1975 [1973]) *The Mirror of Production*. Trans. Mark Poster. St. Louis: Telos Press.

(1981 [1973]) *For a Critique of the Political Economy of the Sign*. Trans. Charles Levin. St. Louis: Telos Press.

(1993 [1976]) *Symbolic Exchange and Death*. Trans. Iain Grant. London: Sage

(1983) *Simulations*. Trans. Paul Foos, Paul Patton, and Philip Beitchman. New York: Semiotext(e).

(1983) *In the Shadow of the Silent Majorities*. Trans. Paul Foss, John Johnston, and Paul Patton. New York: Semiotext(e).

(1983) "The Ecstasy of Communication," in *The Anti-Aesthetic*, ed. Hal Foster. Washington: Bay Press.

(1988) *America*. Trans. Chris Turner. London: Verso.

(1988) *The Ecstasy of Communication*. Trans. Bernard and Caroline Schutze. New York: Semiotext(e).

(1990) *Cool Memories*. Trans. Chris Turner. London: Verso.

(1990) *Fatal Strategies*. New York: Semiotext(e).

(1994) *Simulacra and Simulation.* Trans. Sheila Glaser. Ann Arbor: Minnesota University Press.

(1995) *The Gulf War Did Not Take Place.* Trans. Paul Patton. Sydney: Power Publications.

(1996) *The Perfect Crime.* Trans. Chris Turner. London and New York: Verso Books.

(2000) *The Vital Illusion.* New York: Columbia University Press.

(2002) *The Spirit of Terrorism: And Requiem for the Twin Towers.* Trans. Chris Turner. London: Verso.

(2002) *Screened Out.* Trans. Chris Turner. London: Verso.

(2003) *Passwords.* Trans. Chris Turner. London: Verso.

(2005) *The Intelligence of Evil or the Lucidity Pact.* Trans. Chris Turner. Oxford: Berg.

(2005) *The Conspiracy of Art.* New York: Semiotext(e).

References

Foster, H. (ed.) (1983) *The Anti-Aesthetic: Essays on Postmodern Culture.* Port Townsend, WA: Bay Press.

Norris, C. (1992) *Uncritical Theory: Postmodernism, Intellectuals and the Gulf War.* London: Lawrence and Wishart.

Poster, M. (1988) *Jean Baudrillard: Selected Writings.* Stanford, CA: Stanford University Press.

Turner, C. (2005) Introduction, in: *The Intelligence of Evil or the Lucidity Pact.* Trans. Chris Turner. Oxford: Berg.

Wolin, R. (2004) *The Seduction of Unreason.* Princeton, NJ: Princeton University Press.

3

Baudrillard, Death, and Cold War Theory

Ryan Bishop

The whole art of politics today is to whip up popular indifference.

Jean Baudrillard, *Cool Memories II*, 16

Today there is a growing resemblance between the business mentality and sober critical judgment, between vulgar materialism and the other kind, so that it is at times difficult properly to distinguish between subject and object. . . . To identify culture solely with lies is more fateful than ever, now that the former is really becoming totally absorbed by the latter, and eagerly invites such identification in order to compromise every opposing thought.

Theodor Adorno, *Minima Moralia*, 44

This beer isn't a beer, but that is compensated for by the fact that this cigar isn't a cigar either. If this beer wasn't a beer and this cigar really was a cigar, then that would be a problem.

Bertold Brecht, quoted by Baudrillard,
The Gulf War Did Not Take Place, 81

Embers of the Cold War

Jean Baudrillard can rightfully be described as a Cold War philosopher. He is a philosopher who came to intellectual maturity during the Cold War, and he is a philosopher of all that is and stems from the Cold War.[1] He is a philosopher and analyst of the theories, systems, technologies, methods, and materials of the Cold War, which have affected and infected every aspect of every life that has come into contact with them. In his substantial body of theoretical engagement, he examines the Cold War as the event that has most shaped our current moment and our commonsense understanding of the world and how it works. His language is that of Cold War planners; his logic, that of Cold War strategists; his rhetoric, that of Cold War politicians. In all instances, he has pushed these to their most extreme point, a tendency that he decisively reveals as inherently operative in the processes themselves, and each element of his thought can be returned to the problematics that constitute the Cold War. Baudrillard mainly differs from his Cold War interlocutors in that he occupies the space of Death lurking inside all these systems, theories, and discourses, the Death that undoes their drives for perfection and completion, the Death the Cold War peddlers hawk but deny is part of their wares.

The logic of and ideals/goals represented by US global strategy during the Cold War play essential roles in Baudrillard's theoretical work: from pre-emption to the impossible exchange (another term for détente), to enclosed systems of symbolic exchange to simulation, from consumerism (the most visible portion of the West's economic and political system) to America (as a self-generated and self-generating concept only marginally aligned with its physical space), from technological/media-driven utopian dreams of complete long-distance surveillance and control to containment (the primary goal of US military and diplomatic intervention in relation to the Soviet Union). Clearly, Baudrillard's most famous theoretical concept, the simulacrum, derives directly from his decades-long engagement with simulation and its many effects. Simulation is the *sine qua non* of the Cold War. "The nuclear," as Baudrillard asserted, is "the apotheosis of simulation" (*Simulacra and Simulation*,

32). But the nuclear was made possible by simulation as much as vice versa. For Baudrillard, simulation becomes one of the most significant organizing structures of and concepts for the West, as well as all that has been "globalized," as we move further away from World War II.

As a primary, if not *the* primary, goal of research and development fields, simulation emerges near the end of World War II, and comes into its own under the aegis of Vannevar Bush, who oversaw the US commitment to maintaining its military-industrial superiority in the immediate post-WWII, early Cold War moment by convincing the federal government that it was in its national security interests to do so. Rather than scaling back the standing army and the mobilization of the combined forces of the federal government, the corporate sector, and the university in the service of the military, as was done at the end of World War I, Bush argued that the US should intensify these collaborations while the US still held an advantage over all other nations, especially the Soviet Union. Bush foresaw a coming conflict with the USSR and argued that World War II had occurred primarily because the US had been remiss in its unique position post-World War I. To achieve these aims, Bush directed several programs that brought increasing interaction between university-based research, US government national funding of this research, and close collaboration between private industry in the commercialization of the results of this research, all of it in the service of the military and national defense.

This interaction birthed the heyday of the cognitive sciences and the era of social science specialists who could provide charts and graphs meant not to describe but rather predict human behavior in a given situation. Essential to this predictive capacity of social science research is the model or the simulation. In this manner, events can be modeled ahead of time, predicted, and therefore, if desired, brought to fruition or terminated. In the simulation, then, resides a means by which the pre-emptive strike could be considered, implemented, and justified. The logic of the pre-emptive strike is an essential dimension of the Cold War, and its continued presence finds form in the rationale of the Iraq War, as well as this larger strategy of pre-empting any event that might destabilize globalization and global values. Deterrence becomes a replacement for war, a simulation of war (*Simulacra and Simulation*, 32). At one level, such a situation could be deemed desirable, but could only be so if it actually lessened the chance of armed conflict. In fact, the simulation of war only heightens the chances of such violence occurring, for war (i.e. real, all-out war, with nuclear missiles flying across continents) remains impossible. And instead of war, the world has witnessed multiple smaller but incredibly bloody and brutal conflicts. In addition, any chance of so-called "rogue" states acquiring the nuclear capacity that only the "rational" regimes of the West should possess would mean an unleashing of the impossible exchange, and thus provides justification for pre-emption, as we have already witnessed. The link between the desirability of predictive thinking and pre-emptive action insofar as it pertains to the current conflict in Iraq is taken up by Baudrillard when he states, "The ultimate reason [for the war] is to create a securitized order, a general neutralization of peoples on the basis of the final nonevent" ("Mask"). In terms of its larger and longer implications, he argues that "it is going to be necessary, then, to invent a security system that prevents any event from occurring. A whole strategy of deterrence that does service today for a global strategy" (*Intelligence of Evil*, 118).

Bringing his arguments back to their Cold War roots, Baudrillard asks "Is [this global deterrence] a remnant of the Cold War and the balance of terror? But this time it's a deterrence without cold war, a terror without balance. Or rather it is a universal cold war, ground into the tiniest interstices of social and political life" (*Intelligence of Evil*, 119). The political regimes that hold sway over the global order of globalization processes sprang from Cold War concerns of control and containment. Thus they rely heavily on simulation to model that which needs (in a virtual future yet to be actualized and which must be prevented realization) those situations or events requiring pre-emption, in accord with this logic and its self-preservation. Thus the political curtailed dramatically its purview just when its overall reach expanded to all parts of the globe. General MacArthur's famous Cold War assertion that "We [the US] defend everyplace" has come to mean we defend our simulacral creation and projection of the real everywhere all the time, and that anything that stands outside of it therefore stands against it. To make these desires thinkable, as well as desirable and conceivably achievable, the whole battery of virtuality must be deployed as simulation paves the way for pre-emption.

Simulation itself came to define the vast majority of what constituted university-based research in the Cold War because so much of it was driven by the defense-spending nexus organized by Bush. In the area of simulation, this tight nexus of governmental (that is, defense-driven) research conducted in laboratories based in US universities (MIT, in the initial instance) and the private sector (IBM and American Airlines) can be clearly articulated. The first simulated environments created at MIT were designed almost simultaneously for defense purposes and business needs: SAGE (semi-automated ground environment) and SABRE (semi-automated business research environment). With SAGE, operators of weapons tracking and aiming devices could use a "light gun" to identify objects that appeared on their screens, allowing weapons to be directed according to the operators' understanding of the environment as displayed on their screens and not within their empirical fields of vision. The simulation of the airspace environment under the operators' jurisdiction allowed air defense to be conducted at a distance and from a desk, not out in the field.

With the knowledge garnered from SAGE, MIT almost immediately started SABRE, a system designed by IBM for American Airlines to link thousands of reservations clerks throughout the country in a shared system of online transaction processing. The simulated environment made it possible for data, information, and purchases to be exchanged in real time as if all the reservation clerks were sitting in the same room. The power of simulation to affect and control other spaces grew to be an integral part of the Cold War world, especially when war games were actuated allowing military planners to work through a variety of nuclear warfare scenarios while keeping the Cold War cold − or so they hoped and believed. The long-term, long-range, unforeseen effects of simulation in all areas of existence become one of the major sites of analytic concentration for Baudrillard, and for obvious reasons.

Large-scale simulation, Baudrillard argues, ushers in the third order of the simulacra, in which there is no difference between the accurate representation of reality and the manufactured one. And with the third order of simulacra, all means of traditional political resistance and action have been rendered irrelevant. "Contemporary revolutions," he writes in 1976, "are indexed on the immediately prior state of the system. They are all buttressed by a nostalgia for the resurrection of the real in all its forms, that is, as second-order simulacra: dialectics, use-value, the transparency and finality of production, the 'liberation' of the unconscious, of repressed meaning (the signifier, or the signified named "desire") and so on" (*Symbolic Exchange and Death*, 3). Baudrillard continues his argument about the futility of traditional modes of political action claiming that the mobilization of "third-order simulacra sweeps [these modes] away" and would only lead to political regression. "You can't fight the aleatory by imposing finalities," he argues, "you can't fight against programmed and molecular dispersion with *prises de conscience* and dialectical sublation, you can't fight the code with political economy, nor with 'revolution'" (ibid.). The "higher-order system," that enacted by third-order simulacra, "neutralizes" all these "outdated weapons" (ibid.). Such analyses prove harsh for those, especially in the West, seeking political change, and Baudrillard's words are largely unheard or misunderstood by those who carry the banner of Enlightenment progress, political justice, and civic representation. And yet, it is impossible to ignore the fact that American *Realpolitik* dismissed the millions who protested around the world – on TV, in the streets, on the Internet – prior to the invasion of Iraq to no effect whatsoever: outdated weapons indeed. That these demonstrations merely perform political participation – merely simulate politics – stunningly reinforces Baudrillard's analysis of the diminished status of the political subject and its agency. That the second Bush administration managed to be re-elected, further erodes the sense of majority representation as a part of the democracy promoted around the world by the powers that have created and maintain global values.

The global, as we have come to know it, directly results from Cold War logic, strategies, and systems. The goal of complete, "real time" surveillance of the entire earth transforms this sphere of ours from a planet to a globe, capable of being held in a tele-technological hand and surveyed from all sides at all times all the time. In order to achieve the dream of being able to see everything that unfolds on the face of the globe as it occurs (that is, in real time), a host of technologies and strategies have been deployed, modified, and updated – tele-technologies and opto-electronics, as well co-ordinated large-scale computing systems, that not only seem to realize the goal of complete real-time surveillance but also help to make us believe that the goal is realizable. The abbreviation for this process begun in the 1950s is C^{3}I, which stands for communication, control, containment, and information. In C^{3}I resides the seeds of what becomes later, in Baudrillard's term for the global regime of neoliberal democracy and the tools deployed to deliver it, Integral Reality. C^{3}I itself has been repeated and intensified in C4ISTAR (command, control, communications, computers, intelligence, surveillance, target acquisition, and reconnaissance).

An important aspect of Integral Reality is also an important aspect of C^{3}I: the desire to render all phenomena transparent, visible, known. As Baudrillard clearly articulates the current situation, "Integral Reality is the perpetrating on the world of an unlimited operational project whereby everything becomes real, everything becomes visible and transparent, everything is 'liberated,' everything comes to fruition and has a meaning (whereas it is in the nature of meaning that not everything has it)" (*Intelligence of Evil*, 17). For the US during the Cold War, everything everywhere at all times had potential influence on the state of its security. Similarly with Integral Reality "there is no longer anything on which there is nothing to say" (ibid.). In this drive to realize everything as transparent, or the real, an omnipotent form of subjectivity and agency also emerges, one that believes itself beneficently in control of the technology. As Baudrillard warns, the belief in subject agency when it comes to technology is a byproduct of the technology and technicity itself. Thus the effect is confused as a cause.

In the 1980s, Baudrillard begins to refer to the masses – that great foundational trope of social analysis and justification for political action – as "the silent majority." This terminology proves rather witty, borrowing as it does from Richard Nixon, who used it to describe a presumed but unarticulated consensus opinion held by the US population and not aired in public arenas, as student anti-Vietnam War protesters did. Nixon's phrase is an unwitting allusion to Homer, who used it in reference to the dead (the dead outnumber the living and remain silent despite their great numbers). Baudrillard's use of the phrase cuts in a number of directions, largely those signaling the demise of the political subject and the empty sign that the masses have become due to the effects of simulation and abstraction meted out in Cold War technicity. Baudrillard argues that the masses can no longer participate in the order of representation – that their voices have yielded to the survey, their self-reflexivity swallowed by endless institutional tests. Such tools as polls, referenda, tests, surveys, etc., he argues, "no longer belong to the domain of representations, but to one of simulation" (*In the Shadow of the Silent Majorities*, 20).

The fate of the masses and that of the individual that constitutes the masses are explicitly intertwined. The masses used to be considered collectively a subject themselves, much as the individuals who form it were. Both have been rendered silent, a position designed for them but which also holds further unintended consequences. "Withdrawn into their silence," Baudrillard asserts, "they are no longer (a) *subject* (especially not to – or of – history), hence they can no longer be spoken for, articulated, represented" (*In the Shadow*, 22). The silence of the silent majority as a collective entity echoes the silence of the subject as individual agent. Outside of history, both the mass subject and the individual subject have been abstracted into a position of apathy created by bureaucratic and centralized power, only, according to Baudrillard, to have this self-same apathy become an inertia powerful enough to undermine the very systems that rendered them null and void. In response to another but deeply implicated political agenda, the War on Terror, Baudrillard describes his project in a fashion that links directly to the demise of the political subject, the import of simulation in its end, the role of the Cold War for our current moment, and the ineluctable obstacles confronting the impulse for all-inclusive, self-perfecting systems of domination, when he says "I have endeavored to analyze the process through which the unbounded expansion of globalization creates the conditions for its own destruction" ("Fourth World War").

A story of the subject

Baudrillard's work consistently examines the effects of media and tele-technologies – all of which play integral roles in the influence of simulation – on the system of identity largely held to be "common sense" in much of the modern world: the subject–object relationship. The self, in this relationship, is a subject gazing on and interacting with a world of objects (including other selves or subjects), thus knowing itself through its interactions with and differences from these objects. This system of identity emerges from a specific set of cultural-historical parameters and is deeply implicated in an array of other, related systems of thought and institutions, e.g. subjectivity, agency, empowerment, self-determination, and autonomy. The grammatical construction in many Western languages of subjects and objects is reflected in the semantic categories of subjects and objects, which in turn unfolds into and reflects theories of self and other, justice, nation-state, systems of governance, ethics, political economy, and taxonomies of nature.

The entire apparatus of the subject–object relationship, so Baudrillard argues, has been threatened, if not actually rendered a wistful remembrance of inheritances past, by the battery of technologies and technicities that help create contemporary conditions. Though still apparently vibrant in its manifest circulation of the globe in the form of default "universal" values espoused by hegemonic nations and economies in the post-Cold War world, the subject–object relation exists only in the form of a simulation of what it might once have been. It hangs on as if by magic, or by the magic of "as if" – that is, "as if" the dialectic between subject and object, or the true and the false, the useful and the useless, etc. still retained validity in the face of globalization processes and their various technologies for delivering the global.

Taking the place of the subject–object relationship is what Baudrillard calls a network–screen relationship, in which subjects and objects are replaced by screens for the transmission and reception of ideas, images and information, and networks for the delivery of them. Subjects and objects, he writes, have been "screened out," along with a number of other paired phenomena dependent upon distance, including the real and simulation, as well as the written text and its virtual avatar (*Screened Out*, 176–80). The gaze of the subject upon a world of objects in which a scene or a spectacle transpires has yielded to screens tapped into vast networks that result in a kind of fascination and complete obscenity. The distance necessary for subjects to observe, engage, manipulate, and differentiate themselves from objects has been swallowed up by tele-technologies whose sole purpose of existence is to erase the gap of perception. They have been so successful, Baudrillard argues, that the gap has gone, leaving only screens in networked relation with one another without difference. Having striven for perfection and total completion in the elimination of the gap between subject and object, these tele-technologies, in their manifest achievement, have left no difference between subject and object, self and other, here and there, to the point of their elimination.

But it is not technology alone that has brought this situation about, but rather technology in accord with a changing set of relationships that technology both helps produce and intensifies. There is a complex set of interactions between tele-technologies, media, advertising, consumerism, and capitalism that all operate under a few important shared attributes and conditions. The first and most important of these is abstraction. The overriding justification for the expansion of systems generally in the West after World War II remains efficiency, speed, autonomy, and profit with technology both as object and idea (or abstraction) being the vehicle to deliver the abstracted essence of production and functionality. But, as noted above, the drive for completion and total perfection has resulted in the death of the very systems that produce functionality and abstraction, as well as the death of functionality and abstraction themselves. Similarly the subject as political actor, agent, and object dies. Death becomes the most intractable object, the last intractable object, and its errant intractability might well be our salvation, if Baudrillard is to be believed.

The island of lost selves, or the audience

To get a sense of how Baudrillard's views resonate with specific trends operating in the public discursive sphere, one only needs to turn to one of his favorite and most fecund sources of cultural production for the global: Hollywood. The 2005 Hollywood release entitled *The Island* offers the usual cocktail of technology-based fears, along with the technological and humanistic solutions to those fears, on which Hollywood thrives. At its most basic level, the plot evokes the anxiety of agency in a fully mediated, militarized, and biotechnologically determined world. Set in the not too distant future, which means the present of course, Ewan McGregor and Scarlett Johansson play clones being raised for organ culling, a service provided by a maniacal mega-medical corporation with obscure US Defense Department links for the perpetuation of life for the ultra-wealthy. In order for the organs to function effectively, we are told, the clones must possess some semblance of individuality, a shadow of subjectivity, including the simulations of memory and a past. To keep the clones docile and well-managed, each one is force-fed a false global history of whole-scale environmental disaster, the fallout from which would kill anyone who left the protective biosphere world they inhabit – a post-apocalyptic simulation easily carried off due to the massive exposure to such scenarios in films, government drills, novels, and TV. The biosphere world where the clones are housed, not surprisingly, resembles the generic mall in which most multiplex cinemas are contained. The external world they see out of their windows is a computer-generated hologram of urban contamination and decay to further dupe the clones. The McGregor and Johansson clones develop an unexpected and problematic capacity for curiosity and knowledge. They flee their sealed world (they are referred to as "product on the loose" by the corporate baddies) and enter the near-futural human cities of New York City and Los Angeles. The cinematic representations of these cities look strikingly like the hologram world that has been projected to the clones, only a bit cleaner and with nifty mass transport.

These cities and the hologram also look strikingly like the computer-generated tag of skyscrapers complete with broadcast screens as facades that accompany the series of ads before the film starts, a sequence provided by and for a company called Mediatech, which provides advertising trailers shown before movies in Singapore. The cinematic cities portrayed in *The Island* also bear a strong resemblance to the Isetan/Shaw brothers' tower on Orchard Road, in Singapore, which houses one of the more popular local cineplexes. The cinema audience, clones, and humans alike – diegetic and non-diegetic – all find themselves embedded in a multilayered urbanscape of mediated, commodified, broadcast simulation. The urban real has been swallowed by the hyperreal of cinema both within the content of the film and the context of watching it. The separation between representation and production has been erased.

The mediation, though, goes much further as the film engages in one of Hollywood's favorite topics: the thematizing of cinema and its relationship with its audience. Much of this thematizing occurs in the form of anxiety about cinema's power over its audience, but it is always expressed with deep ambivalence (with cinema simultaneously proud of its power and concerned about it). When the nascent clones are being provided memory inserts to construct a past, we see them strapped to medical operating tables with computer monitors flashing their simulated, pre-programmed pasts, each one with his/her individual screen ("*my* past" in website-speak, reminding us of "*my* favorites" on Windows Internet prompts or "*my* wish list" on Amazon). The scene looks like a huge warehouse filled with an endless phalanx of Frankenstein's monsters, or Alexes from *A Clockwork Orange*, a repetition of cinematic anxieties past intensified in quantity and technological sophistication. As the clones receive these memory inserts, we see them twitching and squirming in mechanical response to the simulation of a past broadcast directly to each individual clone, to which we, the audience, respond with our own twitches and squirms caused by the visual and aural input of the film and *its* simulation of our collective future-present.

The method of instruction and the source of anxiety are the same: i.e. cinema, which evokes metonymically media, technology, communication models, urban space, and consumer culture. From the diegetic world of cinematic narrative to the non-diegetic world of the audience, thematized at every level is the power of simulation, with the cinema, the mall and the urbanscape being both cause for and solution of anxieties surrounding individual agency. The beautiful clones played by McGregor and Johansson, as one can anticipate, provide us with one of the main messages of the film: how to be human in such a fully technologically determined environment. In other words, the clones show the audience that *they* are more human than the dehumanized humans they replicate and who have put in requests for their manufacture and ultimate destruction. In this manner, the simulation teaches us, yet again, what it means to be human, which now equates with being technologically manufactured as clones, films, movie stars, and models. The simulation of the human found in the clone, the star, the model, the film, etc. tells a story of subjectivity and agency lost but potentially regained, but *only* through the simulation and medium that have revealed this information to us. In a similar fashion, the simulation of war found in the Gulf War, which is that of war as TV, and the simulation of war operative in the Iraq War, which is that of war as film, reveal to us the end of international geopolitical action available in the recent past. Though the losses seem to be of different magnitudes and desirability, they essentially are the same and reflect the same anxiety. The central anxiety concentrates on the degree to which agency and individuality are possible, if at all, when space and self (even the collective self of a political entity) are so materially and immaterially altered by a host of technologies and technics. If cinema is endlessly fascinated and appalled by its power, as it is, and if cinema also displays an anxiety about itself as a lost object (which is why it thematizes itself over and over again), then it merely replicates and perpetuates the loss of the subject manifested by its audience, which is the result of its interaction with its audience.

While we have barely begun to scratch the analytic surface of this typical example of Hollywood product on the loose, it is worth mentioning the role of desire and sexual attraction upon which Hollywood and consumer culture so depend and which they manufacture. In the global market, sexuality and desire become standard-bearers for the site in which individuality and agency are most uniquely articulated. We are told that the clones

are kept ignorant of sex and desire (that "they are like fifteen-year-
olds"!), and when the beautiful clone couple are on the run, we
see them innocently asleep in deserted buildings, like children in
Edenic bliss. The Johannson clone, however, is a clone of a famous
model, rather like Johansson herself, and the couple encounter
images of desire and lust for the first time when they see a perfume
ad featuring her human original broadcast in the lobby of a department store in New York City. The ad within the film performs
just as global media and consumer culture perform outside the film
– if we can maintain this distinction – by creating the twitch of
sexual desire in the form of famous, fully simulated and commodified desirable bodies. For the beautiful clones in the film, though,
learning about sex through advertising becomes a liberating and
empowering experience, outside the realm of mediated anxiety
about selfhood and agency. The agency of the self emerges only in
and through the fully commodified urbanscape provided by media
(e.g. the trailer of ads, the cinema, the mall, the city street). To
add to the *mise-en-abime* of fully thematized and mediated experience, we – the audience I was a part of – see the same ad the clone
couple sees (via a bit of product placement by Calvin Klein) when
it is projected in the Mediatech series of commercials prior to the
screening of the film. The mobius strip of media articulation folds
in and out of itself, leaving no inside or outside for the audience to
negotiate. Urban space, consumerism, media, broadcast, and technology converge on the vulnerable notions of agency through and
as the constructs of desire. The distance required for subjects and
objects to engage one another as such disappears into the strident
articulation of screen–network relations.

Simulation and pre-emption: subduing
the event (yet again)

Extending a conceit borrowed from Francois de Bernard, itself a
continuation of his own conceit, Baudrillard writes that the Iraq
War is a film: not *like* a film – not a simile – but film itself (rather
like the Gulf War *is* TV). The Iraq War has a "screenplay" which
"has to be fulfilled unerringly" (*Intelligence of Evil*, 124). Everything

from technical to financial materiel, including control of distribution (similar to Charlie Chaplin, Mary Pickford, and Douglas
Fairbanks with their United Artists studio), has been mobilized
for "The Iraq War: The film." "In the end," Baudrillard argues,
"operational war becomes an enormous special effect; cinema
becomes the paradigm of warfare, and we can imagine it as 'real,'
whereas it is merely the mirror of its cinematic being" (ibid.).
The audience of the Iraq War, in all of its modes of delivery and
distribution, then replicate the audience of *The Island*. The implications of this replication at the level of the political become rather
obvious, but not necessarily so at first glance. If the audience of
The Island witnesses a self on screen no longer accessible to them
other than on screen, then the audience of the Iraq War witnesses
political action (technological, military, and economic) no longer
accessible to constituents of representational government other
than onscreen. As noted earlier, even those arenas usually allotted
to the general populace in representational governments have been
subsumed by the drive to Integral Reality as exemplified by the
global demonstrations against the invasion of Iraq that did nothing
to slow the attack and only filled up TV news shows with the
performance of dissent. The result is, according to Baudrillard, that
"we are henceforth dealing with the exercise of power in the pure
state with no concern for sovereignty or representation; with the
Integral Reality of negative power" (*Intelligence of Evil*, 120).

More worrying, however, might be the relationship between
the simulation of cinematic experience of the Iraq War and its relationship to the drive toward Integral Reality, as delineated in *The
Intelligence of Evil*, but foreshadowed briefly in the Gulf War essays.
The key connections here are those that link simulation (or modeling) to pre-empting any phenomena, set of values, or actions that
might lead to an event, a disruption of the drive to completion of
the Real: here understood as the platitudes operating under terms
such as universal values, democracy, neoliberal economic markets,
etc. The entire apparatus of globalization processes intends to
perfect and complete the Real and the Good on its own terms and
with Universal Values as its justification. The relationship between
the global and the universal replicates that between technics and
truth.

The Gulf War essays show how the fully mediated simulacral conflict of the early 1990s fit the larger pattern of Cold War deterrence as another means of waging conflict and thus realizing as completely as possible the control of images and information (disinformation). On the geopolitical scale, then, the purpose of wars is to rein in recalcitrant regimes while sending messages to other potential foes about the technological, military, and simulational power of the US: "the large footprint" in the sand that the Pentagon invoked during the early period of the Iraq War. Sending a message, of course, has long been a strategy for exercising sovereignty. About the Gulf War, Baudrillard writes, "Our wars have less to do with the confrontation of warriors than with the domestication of the refractory forces on the planet, those uncontrollable elements as the police would say, to which belong not only Islam in its entirety but wild ethnic groups, minority languages, etc. All that is singular and irreducible must be reduced and absorbed. This is the law of democracy and the New World Order" (*Gulf War*, 86). This is, of course, the project of simulation, the wresting of the event *in potentia* from its potential and potential realization. The model and the object merge to create one whole entity, as in the third order of simulacra. Containment leads not just to control but also to osmosis, to preventive measures rendering any further or similar outbreaks possible. And all of it scripted ahead of time. The script demands that nothing deviate from the script, a screenplay writer with some real clout at last.

The raw power of the integral drive is based, in Baudrillard's argument, entirely on "the prevention and policing of events" (*Intelligence of Evil*, 121), to fulfill the script's demands. This, after all, was the justification for the pre-emptive nature of the Iraq War, whose aim was nominally the *prevention* in advance of Saddam's use of weapons of mass destruction. The models provided by intelligence and tele-technological surveillance indicated variance from the global order of Integral Reality and thus necessitated, in simplistic cause-effect rationalization, the preventive measure known as war – but only war that is cinema: scripted, special effects, everything all in place and safe when the lights go up. But the prevention now is universal, absolute, no longer contained to war or security. "Anything that could happen," Baudrillard argues, "anything that might take place is regarded as terrorism. The rule, or the order, is that nothing can take place, nothing is to occur any more. So anything that can occur must be predicted in advance, exterminated in advance" (Hegarty, 2004: 147). And this is what war has become: pre-emption, carrying Cold War logic to its complete and completely (il)logical ends of absolute completion. Everything is a threat that does not emerge from the order that controls the spread of Integral Reality. Terrorism is "no longer at all religious or ideological . . . it's all forms. So, in practice, it's total war, maybe the fourth world war, or like Virilio said, a sort of planetary civil war, as it's a coalition of all powers on the side of order against all those who are potential terrorists. All populations are virtually terrorist insofar as they have not been exterminated" (ibid.).

Baudrillard's analyses, rather like the Cold War doctrine that maintained an enforced state of terror called mutually assured destruction (MAD), might seem to leave us no room for maneuvering or action of any kind. Yet, Death lurks in the systems he discusses, the ones driving incessantly to completion and perfection, and Death provides us hope, though, admittedly, a slim one. The systems generate their own modes of destruction, an auto-destructivity that emerges from the very processes that wish to exclude any resistance to them. In an exceptionally prescient passage that can be linked directly to the Iraq War, Baudrillard asserts:

> But this Integral Reality of power is also its end. A power that is no longer based on anything other than the prevention and policing of events, which no longer has political will but the will to dispel ghosts, itself becomes ghostly and vulnerable. Its virtual power – its programming power in terms of software and the like – is total, but as a result it can no longer bring itself into play, except against itself, by all kinds of internal failures. At the height of its mastery, it can only lose face. (*Intelligence of Evil*, 121)

The loss of face Baudrillard evokes here is not the result of hubris, per se, but rather the effect of realizing exactly what one has set out to achieve. The hermitic world of complete containment, surveillance, and control, no matter how illusory, if successful, can only

ever result in yielding for itself no outside. Anything that impedes
the spread of this Integral Reality is co-opted or obliterated, which
is the position of "Islam" for the West. In its abstracted, political
sense, "Islam," which must be put in qualifying quotation marks,
materializes that which would and does oppose Integral Reality.
But this materialization will not be the force that undoes the drive
to completion; rather the seeds of its own demise are sown from
within. A drive for utter completion – logically and redundantly
– can only end when it is complete: a kind of systematized self-
destruction through realization. The conditions that make Integral
Reality possible, as well as the goals it desires, therefore render it
impossible to achieve and undesirable to do so. Yet it persists, and
more perniciously than ever, despite the humiliating, bloody and
intractable conflict in Iraq.

The salvation of theory in death, or the salvation that is death

Although death is pivotal to many whose work falls within the
domain of critical theory, Baudrillard's work, perhaps more so than
others', articulates, embodies, and enacts the role of Death within
theoretical writing and its relation to the political. Death, and
especially the death drive in Freud according to Baudrillard, does
not provide any space for the operation of dialectical co-option or
reclamation. And it is this trait, Death's absolute imperviousness
to the dialectic, that makes it radical, intractable, usable (*Symbolic
Exchange and Death*, 151). Such is the position that Baudrillard
himself assumes within analyses of media, simulation, the subject,
the object, politics, war, economics, culture, the event, theory
itself, and thought. In relation to systems, the Death that Baudrillard
wishes to address functions in a two-fold manner: it is what waits at
"the *term* of the system" – at its end – and it is "the symbolic *extermination* that stalks the system itself" (*Symbolic Exchange of Death*, 5).
Therefore Death is both internal to the system and its "operational
logic" and "a radical-finality" outside it. Only Death operates both
within and without the system (5). As such it carries the mark of
perfection (completion of the system's operation and project) and

the defectiveness inherently lurking within it. Death is ambiguity and paradox made manifest, and is both the system's realization and its impediment.

Death resists modeling, the simulation. Its lack of predictability and the difficulty in controlling it, in fact, resides at the center of the various systems, policies, and logics that drive the Cold War. Death is the event without compare and which must be elided at all costs. Under the patriotic yet threatening rubrics of security, safety, "our way of life," etc., the entire elaborate apparatus of the Cold War was erected and launched, while also continuing with intensified reverberations into the present – all to ward off Death on a scale hitherto the domain of Nature or the gods. Following a lead from the poet Octavio Paz and sounding like an interlocutor of Paul Virilio's, Baudrillard discusses Death, therefore, in terms of the accident (*Symbolic Exchange and Death*, 160–6). For as Paz contends, modern science and technology, including medicine, have converted epidemics and natural catastrophes into explainable and controllable phenomena. The rational order can explain and contain anything that threatens it, as can Integral Reality (for which the rational order is another metonym, as is the global). As such, Death becomes an accident to be contained and controlled, explained and predicted. If Death equals an accident, and accidents threaten the rational order, Baudrillard argues, then Death-as-accident also threatens political sovereignty and power, "hence the police presence at the scenes of catastrophe" (161). Death is the disruption that destabilizes all that has been ordered and made stable.

At the height of the Cold War as an historical phenomenon, the major powers relied heavily on a rational order that both players acknowledged (at least between themselves) to be operational. This led to the enforced and heavily armed stalemate of MAD, and with it arrived the horrific spectacle of the nuclear accident, or the computer accident. The accidental launch of the impossible exchange of missiles would be, in rote pronouncements of certitude, "*the only way*" these rational and sane nations would fire nuclear weapons: hence the many examples of cultural representations of accidental nuclear war that filled popular media (invoking worlds synonymous to the one portrayed as the simulated wasteland in *The*

Island). The import of simulation in containing Death on a global scale can be seen in the supposed rational containment of both the opposition and oneself. The simulated scenarios of both war games and accidental launches, the modeling of events, become a kind of necromantic or occult means of controlling unleashed forces and foretelling possible futures in order to prevent the accident (or the event) – to prevent Death itself.

The thought processes, or mental make-up, required to plan and design large-scale modeling meant to pre-empt accidents are themselves a kind of technology of thinking, and this mental technicity comprises an important element in the construction of Integral Reality. Simulation requires faith not in its own verisimilitude but in its capacity to change events, even Death. The US embodies this kind of faith and has from the Cold War to the present, which, as such, becomes a target for many satiric novelists. One particularly influenced by Baudrillard's ideas about simulation is Don DeLillo, whose novel *White Noise* reads like a primer on the French theorist's writings. One motif in the novel is a company called SIMUVAC, which stands for "simulated evacuation." The company stages fake evacuations for a variety of emergencies, including nuclear events, complete with a theatrical or cinematic set of special effects: uniforms, sound effects, smells, and blood (if required). The firm turns up several times in the novel but makes its first, and most satirically poignant, appearance during an actual emergency. In perfect Baudrillardian fashion, the company, which operates solely with and for simulation, uses a live emergency to practice (or simulate) its own simulated emergencies, which is the commodity it packages and sells to various government agencies.

The protagonist of the novel asks a SIMUVAC employee, in the midst of the actual crisis, to evaluate their rehearsal. The SIMUVAC operative replies in darkly comedic fashion:

> The insertion curve isn't as smooth as we would like. There's a probability excess. Plus which we don't have our victims laid out where we we'd want them if this was an actual simulation. In other words we're forced to take our victims where we find them. We didn't get a jump on computer traffic. Suddenly it just spilled out, three-dimensionally, all over the landscape. You have to make allowances for the fact that

everything we see tonight is real. There's a lot of polishing to do. But that's what this exercise is all about. (DeLillo, 1985: 139)

The passage contains beautiful parodic examples of the vagaries that language suffers at the hands of bureaucrats, with nonsense phrases passing as technical jargon, including "insertion curve" and "probability excess," as well as the delightfully oxymoronic "actual simulation." But beyond this parody, DeLillo evokes the technicity of thought deeply embedded in Cold War America, the same technicity that Baudrillard works through at multiple levels, to reveal the deep investment in the power and control afforded by simulation. The desirable element of simulation is, in fact, control, such as with body placement, which is something actual disasters arrange without care or consultation with the modelers. When the SIMUVAC employee claims that things are in need of "polishing" because "everything we see tonight is real," we witness the retreat into the comfortable delusion afforded by simulation despite its no-nonsense claims to hard-nosed pragmatism – "that's what this exercise is all about," he asserts. SIMUVAC, as a company, markets readiness, the capacity to make a community alert and prepared, but can only deliver on this promise as long as everything remains contained in the model. (And if events do not remain neatly in the model, then the company can use the "accident" to better refine their simulation and techniques.) The same is true of governments, and this is the fear of the accident – and the fear the accident manifests – that Baudrillard (*pace* Paz) analyzes. Every sector of Integral Reality lives in fear of events because they can "spill out, three-dimensionally, all over the landscape," no longer in control of the system. All that various institutions, systems, and technologies promise to contain refuses to be contained. Such is the revenge of the object, about which Baudrillard writes, and the intractability of that which lies outside the systems of transparency and integration. Death stalks the protective simulating enterprises from inside and out.

Baudrillard as a stylist of considerable skill and a rhetorician well-steeped in the rhetorical tradition similarly mobilizes his writing itself as Death in relation to the systems operative within academic discourse. From the late 1960s on, his writings and books have deviated rather widely from the conventions of sociological or philosophical genres and academic writing by reaching into the humanistic essay tradition (long since abandoned) and combining it with the most current of pressing issues. What constitutes a standard argument within the humanities and qualitative social sciences, what passes for knowledge and knowledge formation and construction, depends heavily on the adherence of a given work to these conventions. Baudrillard's textual Deaths provide "fatal strategies" intended to stave off the actual death of thought that can result from routinized, by-the-number, knowledge formation. The aphoristic style, borrowed most directly from Nietzsche, works in a nonlinear fashion that nonetheless makes consistent and sustained arguments across his books as well as within them. Baudrillard teases an idea, settles on a problematic, and pulls at its various permutations, checking how it might work from one context to another. As a result, his writing can be simultaneously readable and enjoyable while also being difficult and frustrating. Like his friend Virilio, he does not develop his argument in a full or linear fashion, instead allowing for fragments, tangents, and hyperbole to carry thought off course and place readers in a textual space that is comfortable (especially if they have read nineteenth-century philosophers) and discomfiting at the same time.

To this end, he resurrects outmoded philosophical discourse while at the same time adding to it a late modernist poetic sensibility. The latter quality emerges most obviously in his deployment of terms as talismans of the moment of writing as well as terrain themselves for inquiry: the strategic deployment of labels and phrases intended to make us pay attention to their elasticity and formidable ability to fascinate, illuminate, and instantiate a stability of unstable phenomena. Baudrillard is always contemporary, his thoughts being solidly grounded in the present, and his terminology is always embedded in the current moment. He relies on older essayistic forms to structure his thoughts and musings, which often appear as thoughts and musings, i.e. slightly inchoate and coming into focus through the act of writing. The processual quality of his style injects Death as that which cannot be represented adequately into the deathly regimes of academic language meted out by rote adherence to genre-driven formulae within academic discursive practices.

In an important sense, Baudrillard posits that Death is the salvation of theory while also arguing for the salvation that is Death. With the nuclear sword of Damocles dangling over our heads ever since the explosions at Hiroshima and Nagasaki, we have slipped into a constant state of imminent global death that no longer seems like death, so swift and horrible will it be that it outstrips our imagination. "If the bomb drops," he writes in *America*, "we shall neither have the time to die nor any awareness of dying" (42). Echoing the neo-Freudian psychoanalyst Ernst Becker, Baudrillard argues that Death ostensibly has been removed from our horizon in the American Era, and we, those who follow in America's global footsteps, have moved easily and subtly into a state of daily ease and material comfort, buffeted and protected by a staggering array of tele-technologies, opto-electronics, and international ballistic missiles all meant to keep Death at bay and survival at the forefront. Lost in this heady combination of technological, intellectual, and economic materiel mounted for sheer survival, of course, is life (43). Only that which is alive can die, and our cocooned embrace of globalization, which in turn cocoons and embraces us, leaves us with an existence that recalls the prescient horror films of George Romero begun early in the Cold War: an existence like that of zombies, neither alive nor dead, but frantically and brainlessly consuming all in sight.

Baudrillard rescues Death from its purgatorial condition of "the not alive" or mere survival. And in order to do so, he takes his cue from the masses who are the targets of this weaponry and way of life, the enactors of this ethos of bland avoidance and unthinking consumption. Their wholesale passivity to the apparatus of survival – from nuclear bunkers to Star Wars – emerges from a weariness of having been ceaselessly confronted with apocalyptic visions since the first nuclear explosions in New Mexico and Japan, and they "defend themselves with a lack of imagination" (*America*, 44). "The masses' silent indifference to nuclear pathos (whether it comes from the nuclear powers or from antinuclear campaigners) is therefore a great sign of hope," he asserts, "and a political fact of great import" (44). To understand Death as immanent within the system and without it, as immanent within *bios* and *zoe* and without it, is to resist the simulation of Death that hovers over our heads in the Cold War and the War on Terror. The salvation of Death, which is also the salvation of Baudrillard's writing, thought, and analyses, provides us with the means of getting this specific brutal excess back into our collective frame of reference, not for the sake of nihilism, but to resist the nihilism built into all the projects of utter completion and realization that have rendered politics, the subject, the object, thought, and theory as simulation.

Note

1 It should be understood that I am not limiting Baudrillard to a discrete historical event but rather understanding his work in relation to a complex set of trajectories begun prior to World War II and continued after the fall of the Berlin Wall and the demise of the Soviet Union. So the Cold War and its analyses are by no means limited to a determinate time period lost to the past.

References

Baudrillard, Jean (1993 [1976]) *Symbolic Exchange and Death*. Trans. Iain Grant. London: Sage.

Baudrillard, Jean (1990) *Fatal Strategies*. New York: Semiotext(e).

Baudrillard, Jean (1994) *Simulacra and Simulation*. Trans. Sheila Faria Glaser. Ann Arbor, MI: University of Michigan.

Baudrillard, Jean (1995) *The Gulf War Did Not Take Place*. Trans. Paul Patton. Sydney: Power Publications.

Baudrillard, Jean (2002) *Screened Out*. Trans. Chris Turner. London: Verso.

Baudrillard, Jean (2005a) *The Intelligence of Evil or the Lucidity Pact*. Trans. Chris Turner. Oxford: Berg.

Baudrillard, Jean (2005b) "The Mask of War," *C Theory* (www.ctheory. net). Trans. Alex Barder, November 2005.

DeLillo, Don (1985) *White Noise*. New York: Penguin.

Der Spiegel (2004) "This is the Fourth World War: The *Der Spiegel* interview with Jean Baudrillard" (http://www.ubishops.ca/BaudrillardStudies/spiegel.htm) *International Journal of Baudrillard Studies*, 1, 1, January 2004.

Hegarty, Paul (2004) "Interview with Jean Baudrillard" in Paul Hegarty, *Live Theory*. London and New York: Continuum.

Film

The Island (2005) Dir. Michael Bay.

4

Swan's Way: Care of Self in the Hyperreal[1]

Mark Poster

Reality media

As the last century came to an end and the new one began, media culture in the United States has taken increasingly surprising turns toward "reality." On the *Jerry Springer* show ordinary folk reveal and act out their loves and hates before a national television audience. Broadcasting in talk radio format, Howard Stern insults listeners and guests alike and Rush Limbaugh screams at everyone the wisdom of know-nothing reactionary politics. Judge Judy enacts reality court proceedings and extreme sports shows feature disgusting consumption of bugs and horrific battles. On the Internet, users earn a living by selling virtual characters and weapons for players in massively multiple online role-playing games. Bloggers are perfecting the literary form of the online confessional. The brave new world of reality television, talk radio, and virtual global gaming introduces a fascinating, novel landscape of mediated popular culture. Are we to take these examples as indications of a significant cultural formation or simply an ephemeral passing fad of programmers and audience alike? If it does deserve serious attention, what frameworks of interpretation can be used to decode their meanings?

To render my task a bit more manageable I will narrow my focus to one category of these examples of media culture: cosmetic surgery reality TV shows.[2] Starting in late 2002 with ABC's *Extreme Makeover*, many networks programmed new series that presented run-of-the-mill individuals (almost all women) having their bodies transformed by face lifts, breast enlargements, tummy tucks, liposuction, rhinoplasty, tooth veneers, chin implants – a great assortment of surgeries that promised to alter their bodies into the shape of commonly recognized beauty. These medical procedures became performances visible to television viewers. The market success of *Extreme Makeover* encouraged other networks to come up with their own variations on the theme. FX premiered *Nip and Tuck* in July 2003, a fictional series featuring two cosmetic surgeons. MTV inaugurated *I Want a Famous Face* in March 2004, introducing the celebrity factor: participants modeled their surgeries on the bodies of stars. They challenged doctors to reshape them into the image of their favorite pop idol. Not to be left behind, Fox aired *The Swan* in April 2004, a reality series including a competition in each episode between two women having multiple surgeries and culminating in a grand finale of a beauty contest that selected from the winners of each episode the ultimate woman, the swan. The E! Network came aboard with *Dr. 90210* in July 2004, enhancing the format of cosmetic surgery reality television with the aura of Beverly Hills. Throughout 2004 viewers enjoyed a cornucopia of action with scalpels. The US was not alone in its fascination with these series. In the UK in 2005, for instance, makeover television shows included Channel 5's *Cosmetic Surgery*, Sky One's *Sun, Sea and Silicone* and Channel 4's *10 Years Younger*.

Name of show	Network	First aired
Extreme Makeover	ABC	December 11, 2002
Nip and Tuck	FX	July 22, 2003
The Swan	Fox	April 7, 2004 (Season 1: 10 episodes; Season 2: 9 episodes ending December 20, 2004)
I Want a Famous Face	MTV	March 15, 2004
Dr. 90210	E!	July 11, 2004
UK Makeover Shows 2005		
Cosmetic Surgery	Channel 5	
Sun, Sea and Silicone	Sky One	
10 Years Younger	Channel 4	

One might easily approach these programs as baleful examples of patriarchy, capitalist ideology, neoliberal market culture, excruciatingly bad taste, the deplorable culture of the masses, shameful exploitation, audience manipulation, heterosexual normativity, the postmodern imagination, decadent American civilization, the relentless barrage of images of beauty, consumer narcissism, boredom, a culture of superficial amusement, and so forth.

Yet serious issues are raised by these reality TV series of cosmetic surgery. I shall argue first that they exemplify a form of media culture that carries Baudrillard's concept of the hyperreal to new levels and illustrates a landscape of hitherto unimaginable combinations of humans and information machines. Second, and this is my main concern, I shall inquire if and how these shows illustrate a new variation to Foucault's concept of the care of self.[3] To this end, I shall attempt to extrapolate from these television broadcasts a sense of the place of the media in Foucault's notion of the hermeneutics of the subject. Before turning to these somewhat weighty undertakings I shall attempt to clear a space for the analysis by exploring the case of ORLAN, if only to indicate that cosmetic surgery may be a form of body relation that has uses not completely subsumed under the vagaries of late capitalist culture. After all, body modification is common to human societies throughout history, from circumcision, vaginal infibulations, prosthetic devices (Wills, 1995: 482) and tattooing, to piercing, branding, scarification, laser eye surgery, amputation, bleeding with leeches, dieting, muscle building, and drug taking in all their variations – the list might be extended almost indefinitely. The notion of body as a "natural" or sanctified object that must not be touched or altered under any circumstance is a peculiar conceit of Christian Science and perhaps a handful of other cults and viewpoints.

The case of ORLAN

The example of the French performance artist, feminist and cultural critic, ORLAN, must give one pause before relegating the cultural significance of cosmetic surgery on broadcast media to

Figure 4.1: ORLAN as Saint Teresa
(© ADAGP, Paris and DACS, London 2009)

the trash heap of commodified culture. In the 1960s and 1970s
ORLAN was a political radical and feminist artist, not untypical
of the French version of the New Left. Like Chris Burden who
had an associate shoot him in the arm in a performance in the
1970s, ORLAN's art of cosmetic surgeries in public falls within
the category of body performance that aims to shock the audience
into fresh recognition of the flesh as constructed. As Amelia Jones
argues, many artists, from Carolee Schneemann to Yayoi Kusama,
have presented their bodies in torturous positions and settings,
often nude with gooey substances smeared on their limbs and
torsos (Jones, 1998). It is not a far stretch from these art works to
the performance surgeries of ORLAN, although there are serious
differences between them as well that, for my purposes here, may
be bracketed. One of the similarities with art history is easily noted:
ORLAN's work of 1983, "The Assumption of Saint ORLAN,"
combined the artist posed with one breast exposed and a video
monitor underneath with duplicating images of her body. In this

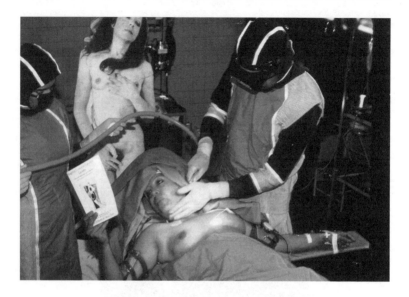

Figure 4.2: ORLAN and Botticelli's Venus
(© ADAGP, Paris and DACS, London 2009)

and other similar projects, ORLAN referenced European art from
earlier periods, such as citing Bernini's *Saint Teresa in Ecstasy* in her
1977 performance "The Kiss of the Artist" (O'Bryan, 2004: 3).

Cosmetic surgery was introduced into her performances with
the project "The Reincarnation of Saint-ORLAN" (1990–1995).
ORLAN's notorious videotaped surgeries were very different
from the widespread practice in the US that is transcoded into television series in the reality TV genre. Her surgeries were intended
as transgressive political statements and also as art works. In the
nineteenth-century tradition of *épater le bourgeoisie* (shock the
middle class), ORLAN's work combines many levels – art history,
feminism, radical politics, poststructuralist theory – as O'Bryan
argues convincingly. The surgeries are informed by facial imagery
of Leonardo Da Vinci's *Madonna*, Sandro Botticelli's *The Birth of
Venus*, and others, incorporating art history, so to speak, into living
flesh. Some scholars are critical of the self-promoting nature of
ORLAN's performances. Carefully produced with Pierre Cardin
accessories and staged for maximum effect, ORLAN is often

regarded as a nutty or even dangerous media opportunist. Yet her performances are also protests against the masculine gaze of heterosexual normativity and commodity culture more generally with their repressive impositions on all genders. Finally, ORLAN's performances enact the critique of foundationalism and naturalism located in the work of Foucault, Derrida, Deleuze, and Lacan, protesting the false assumption of Enlightenment thinking about the body and culture one finds argued so persuasively in English writers such as Judith Butler, Teresa de Lauretis, Elizabeth Grosz, and others. When we turn next to examine cosmetic surgeries in the context of American reality TV, we must bear in mind that these medical procedures, when employed by ordinary people to transform themselves into stereotypes of beauty, continue a line of body performances that explore ways of attending to oneself.

The shows

Each episode of *The Swan* and *I Want a Famous Face* is presented in a rigidly repetitive format. *The Swan* begins with a portrait of each contestant. The contestants are all women in their late 20s to mid-30s. A few are women of color but three-quarters are white. Contestants originate from all over the US from both the middle and working classes. Most have a series of personal problems, ranging from men who left them, low self-esteem, to traumatic events usually in middle school when boys made fun of their appearance. These narratives of suffering and despair are crucial for the drama of the show and the transformation into a swan. Each presents herself as delighted to be chosen to be on the show and determined to become "the swan." Each states that surgery will change their life for the better, solving their numerous problems. Contestants then meet the panel of "experts" who include cosmetic surgeons, dentists, personal trainers, and psychotherapists. The experts consult with the contestant to determine a list of medical procedures that are extensive. The contestants are sequestered during the treatment in a room without a mirror. The procedures begin with the contestant optimistic at first and then devastated by the pain of the surgeries. *The Swan* presents a puritanical code to the contestant: they are being judged by how well they conform to the regimen imposed by the experts.

After recovery, contestants are brought into a heavily decorated room for the "reveal": their first look at themselves since the beginning of the treatment. This is done in front of the experts, the master of ceremonies, and an audience. Everyone is amazed at the physical transformation of the contestant. Compliments abound. The experts are now judges and decide which contestant will proceed to the grand finale that selects "the swan." The primary criterion of judgment is the effort the contestant makes in their transformation, the extent to which they keep to the regimen enunciated by the experts. The winner is not necessarily the most beautiful, whatever that might mean, but the one who struggles hardest for personal redemption. This moral trial is repeatedly announced by the master of ceremonies, leaving no doubt for the audience about the nature of the drama they witness.

I Want a Famous Face has a different but equally rigid format structure. The contestants are younger, mostly in their early 20s. They are more varied: there are some men, some transsexuals, strippers, an Elvis impersonator, in short, people from less conventional lifestyles than on *The Swan*. *I Want a Famous Face* has no voice-overs and no master of ceremonies. It is presented in a documentary and interview style rather than as a contest. The individuals tend to be more savvy and practical about possible results of the surgery than contestants on *The Swan*. They are not in a state of emotional crisis but want to improve their circumstances by having their bodies altered. One wants to impress his girlfriend, another wants a career as a model, another as a singer and performer, and so forth. Participants are not judged by anyone but themselves. Only cosmetic surgeons are used, not personal trainers, psychologists, and the like. A screen flashes the cost of each surgery and the total with the implication – no doubt false – that the participant is paying the bill. *The Swan* also presents an image of each procedure but not the cost incurred. At the outset of the episode a voice-over tells the audience that millions of young people are opting for cosmetic surgery. But in the middle of each episode a two- or three-minute segment features another individual who has undergone the same procedures as the participant but whose life was ruined by them. *The Swan* by contrast presents a wholly upbeat view of cosmetic surgery. Perhaps *I Want a Famous Face* includes the failed surgery as a warning to viewers for insurance purposes. The salient feature of *I Want a Famous Face*, however, is that each participant is a fan of a celebrity who serves as a physical model for their surgery. Participants want a "famous face" or body. Also in contrast with *The Swan* whose contestants are initially presented in the most unfavorable light, without make-up, for example, participants on *I Want a Famous Face* are often quite attractive and their desired "improvements" are far less drastic than contestants on *The Swan*. The former often look something like their idol to begin with.

Other cosmetic surgery reality TV series are slightly different from *The Swan* and *I Want a Famous Face*. But these summaries are enough to indicate the general contours of the genre. We may now attempt to decipher its cultural significance.

Baudrillard's hyperreal

Cosmetic surgery television shows fall within the genre of reality TV. The scholarship on the general issue of reality TV has taken three directions. The first, harking back to the culture industry chapter of Theodor Adorno and Max Horkheimer's *Dialectic of Enlightenment*, finds in it only a new version of the old ideology of the broadcast media; the second, informed by the British cultural studies of Stuart Hall and others, endeavors to complicate the analysis by locating in addition indications of resistance. I shall briefly glance at the positions of each. The third tendency looks to the continuities of recent reality TV with earlier traditions of radio and television that contain many of its elements but did not assume the label. Shows as different as *Queen for a Day* and *Candid Camera*, to mention only two, displayed ordinary people in ways that bridged the gap between the private and the public, between their intimate lives and the mass television audience, much like recent versions of the genre. For reasons that will become clear, this chapter will focus on the first two theoretical tendencies only and leave the historical question of continuity aside.

In the manner of Adorno and Horkheimer, Mark Andrejevic condemns reality TV for its manner of incorporating "interactivity" into broadcast media. The Frankfurt School complained long ago about the monologic nature of broadcast media, sending the same signal to all society with no possibility of audience response. By contrast, Bertolt Brecht (Brecht, 1979–1980) and later Hans Magnus Enzensberger (Enzensberger, 1982) foresaw opportunities for introducing bidirectionality into media and thereby democratizing them. Reality TV, according to Andrejevic, achieves interactivity but does so by intensifying the surveillance of the participants (Andrejevic, 2004). Like the Internet, reality TV promises democracy through interactivity but ends only by strengthening the grip of neoliberal capitalism on the population. While reality TV might appear democratizing, he contends, it only results in "submission to comprehensive forms of monitoring as a form of empowerment and self-expression" (10). Andrejevic sites a cosmetic surgery series in this context: "*Extreme Makeover* neatly combines the double gesture of transforming members of the audience into real television celebrities *while* rebuilding them to fit the conventional image of celebrity beauty" (10). Reality TV is merely one more sham perpetrated by the culture industry on a society that now must conform to the dictates of an "interactive economy." Although he credits himself a "critic" the rhetorical effect of his denunciation of reality TV is not an impetus to struggle but paralysis: nothing can be done that the reigning powers cannot co-opt. Academic cultural studies at the hands of such scholars betray a tendency to refuse any hint of a negative dialectic in popular culture.[4]

The second tendency in reality TV studies is more nuanced. Susan Murray and Laurie Ouellette accept the general direction of the Frankfurt School concern about the commercialization of culture and find tendencies of this in reality TV. But they also attend to the cultural level of the genre and find some ambivalence in its discursive pattern. For them, reality TV

> is an unstable text that encourages viewers to test out their own notions of the real, the ordinary, and the intimate against the representa-

tion before them. Far from being the mind-numbing, deceitful, and simplistic genre that some critics claim it to be, reality TV supplies a multilayered viewing experience that hinges on culturally and politically complex notions of what is real, and what is not. (Murray and Ouellette, 2004: 6)

As a cultural construction of "reality," reality TV unlocks the question of the real at the same time that it attempts to close it. The genre thus opens for the audience the possibility of resistance to the broadcast. With Andrejevic, Murray and Ouellette, noting the surveillance tendencies in the reality TV and in society more generally, conclude that the shows "mitigate" the audience's resistance to such monitoring. Nevertheless they also tentatively acknowledge that reality TV "has spawned an opportunity to wrest control of television images and discourses away from the culture industries" (9).

While these are valuable directions of the analysis of reality TV, neither goes far enough in specifying the cultural form of the media in question. For a grasp of this dimension of the problem, we must turn to the work of Jean Baudrillard. For Baudrillard, media simulate the real rather than represent it. Instead of transcoding the real as in a written or printed text, electronic media appear to duplicate the real directly. What is viewed on television seems to be reality itself. Images and sounds that we perceive in everyday life also appear on the screen (Baudrillard, 1983). Confounding the senses, the screen plays with the real as it is experienced, presenting something that is not the real at all but a simulacrum of it. Baudrillard's point is that the simulacrum is also real but of a different order from everyday life. This different order he names the hyperreal. Media introduce into the cultural landscape something that is not quite real and not quite a representation of the real. What appears on the screen is perceptible but unique. The media, for Baudrillard, always play with their double status as simulation and as reality. In a recent work, he struggles to theorize media hyperreality as a fetish: "So initially, the real object becomes sign: this is the stage of simulation. But in a subsequent stage the sign becomes an object again, but not a real object: an object much further removed from the real than the sign itself – an object off-camera outside representation: a fetish" (Baudrillard, 2001: 129). The media then produce a level of reality that appears as such but is more (and less) than reality.

Baudrillard's lesson for the analysis of reality TV is that the genre is a further complication in the already constituted, unique reality of TV as hyperreal. He writes:

> Even in reality TV, where, in the live telling of the story, in the imme-diate televised acting, we witness the confusion of the existence and its double. No more distance, no more vacuum and no more absence: one enters the screen and the visual image without encountering any obstacle. One enters one's life while walking onto a screen. One puts on one's own life like a digital suit. (Baudrillard, 2005)

In a discussion of the French reality TV show, *The Loft*, Baudrillard, with unconcealed displeasure, interprets reality TV as the apotheosis of the hyperreal. He writes, "Today rather, it would be reality itself which would transfuse en masse into the screen so as to disembody itself there. Nothing any longer separates the screen and the world. The osmosis, the telemorphosis is absolute" (Baudrillard, 2002: 482). The gap between television and reality evaporates in *The Loft*.

Through the use of nonprofessional actors or ordinary folk, reality TV attempts to capture the interest of the audience.[5] Both Andrejevic and Murray/Ouellette report that television audiences find it easier to identify with regular folk than with trained actors. The rapid success of reality TV confirms this hunch. By 2004, reality TV dominated prime-time broadcasting on the major networks. The genre attempts to bring as close as possible the reality of television and reality outside television. Motivated of course by ratings and advertising dollars, television executives are likely to program anything they are allowed in order to achieve success in ratings. The proliferation of reality TV shows no doubt owes much to the pecuniary imperative. Yet the result opens many questions about contemporary popular culture. If reality TV incorporates more and more aspects of extra-television reality, does this change the reality of television? In Baudrillard's terms, is television still hyperreal if it becomes more like extra-television reality? In a show like *Big Brother*, with its broad international success, the camera is placed throughout a living space and simply records what happens. Is the broadcast of such apparent trivia a duplication of the real and therefore different from the hyperreal?

HBO's *The Comeback* (2005) confronts directly the imbrication of the real and the hyperreal. Nominally about the "comeback" of former sitcom star Valerie Cherish (played by Lisa Kudrow), the show fictionalizes reality TV, presenting a fully scripted drama, cast with professional actors, that is staged as a reality TV show. The protagonist is being filmed for a reality TV series but we see the filming itself, making this a double-level reality TV show. Valerie repeatedly requests the director to stop the filming as her misadventures multiply. At yet a third level of self-referentiality, the plot concerns the has-been star auditioning for then filming, you guessed it, a reality TV show. *The Comeback* thoroughly problematizes the genre of reality TV in the process of enacting it at several levels at the same time. Since the plot concerns the fate of a fading celebrity, it also thematizes and puts in question the relation of the movie and television industries to the phenomenon of reality TV.

Critics point out quickly that reality TV is not simply a mimesis of the real. The mediation of the media always changes the signal, always systematically transforms what is in front of the camera and microphone by the machine apparatus. In *Survivor*, for example, the show is elaborately structured: contestants and the setting are carefully chosen; the format emphasizes narrative tension as contestants are voted out by their peers; the promise of remuneration to the winning contestant and possible celebrity for all of them; and so forth. Cosmetic surgery shows are similar in their carefully structured formats. Above all, the images and sounds of the events are recorded and broadcast to be received by televisions in single-family residences, bars, and the like (Spigel, 1992; McCarthy, 2001) beaming the sounds and images to the audience. What might appear to be "reality" remains televised hyperreality. The media effects of the screen do not vanish because the content of the show is "reality."

One might well argue that reality TV is a genre that reflects the current level of media culture, that the "reality" that it incorporates and speaks to is not simply extra-televisual content but as much if not more the generalized dissemination of information machines

in seemingly infinite formats and types. Television is no longer
if it ever was a stand-alone medium of communication. Marshall
McLuhan points out that new media incorporate the content of
older media (McLuhan, 1964). David Bolter and Richard Grusin
argue that new media are for the most part "remediations" of older
media (Bolter and Grusin, 1999). Today I contend the mediascape
(Appadurai, 1996) is a complex of interacting technologies. The
Internet, mobile phones, digital cable and satellite transmissions,
mp3 players, satellite radio – social space is replete with combinations of media that intersect and communicate with one another.
Soap opera fans exchange interpretations of episodes in chat rooms
(Baym, 2000). Young people, armed with mobile phones, send text
messages to friends while tuned in to MTV. In surprising numbers,
the audience for reality TV visit websites related to the shows and
post messages about them. Blogs afford places for the audience to
air their opinions. Computer games become movies (*Lara Croft*;
Grand Theft Auto; *Doom*); TV series become movies (*Starsky and
Hutch*; *The Dukes of Hazzard*) and vice versa (*Bewitched*); radio
shows are televised (Howard Stern); sequels to movies are made by
amateur directors (PanicStruck Productions' *Revelations* as a sequel
to *Star Wars*; fanzines of *Star Trek*); Blogs become books and TV
series (Stephanie Klein's website) – the variations and mixings are
endless. In fact, with images, sounds and texts all digitized, mixing
(sampling, etc.) of cultural objects is the cultural dominant of the
mediascape.

Reality TV is another variation on the theme of intermedia:
the "reality" that is appropriated by the shows is already heavily
mediated. There is not therefore a clean separation between television and reality but an always already mixed blend of the two.
Baudrillard defines the result as a fractal subject:

> In the final stage of his "liberation" and emancipation through the net-
> works, screens and new technologies, the modern individual becomes
> a fractal subject, both subdivisible to infinity and indivisible, closed on
> himself and doomed to endless identity. (Baudrillard, 2001: 47–48)

For him there is no escape from proliferation of information machines and the subjects they constitute. ORLAN, to

Baudrillard, is a symptom not a critique of the current desperate situation: "Everywhere we find the same symbolic mortification . . . The plastic surgery undergone by ORLAN and so many others who experiment on and alter their bodies to the point of mutilation and torture" (49). So advanced is the process of integration between culture and technology that humans are now, in his view, "chimerical cocktails," or "living chimeras, strange mixtures of man and machine" (112). Reality TV then can incorporate only cyborgs, nothing more than the human–machine interfaces that we already are. Before examining the cosmetic surgery shows in relation to Baudrillard's concept of the hyperreal, we must explore Foucault's notion of the care of self.

Foucault's double strategy

If Baudrillard's concept of the hyperreal helps unpack the cultural articulation of the self in the media, especially television, Foucault's writing adds a dimension missing in the analysis thus far: the construction of the body in technologies of power. In *Discipline and Punish* and *The History of Sexuality: Volume 1* Foucault opened the field of study of how the body is implicated in discourses and practices and how these formations are crucial to the cultural figure of the self in a given society. His notions of surveillance through panoptic structures and disciplining through the implementation of norms have proved central to the understanding of reality TV, as we have already seen in the discussion of the work of Andrejevic and Murray/Ouellette. Certainly the self-revealing of individuals on reality TV in general and cosmetic surgery shows in particular, along with Internet modes of self-presentation from Jennycam to personal websites and blogs, constitute forms of surveillance that complicate the carceral context that Foucault analyzed. Today surveillance is extended by video cameras in streets and public buildings but also by the seemingly voluntary public display of personal life in the media. Add to this constellation of exhibitionism the unconscious, unintentional contribution of people to databases through credit card purchases, long-distance and mobile phone calls and we have what I have called a super-panopticon (Poster, 1995). As productive as Foucault's idea of surveillance has become for cultural studies, it remains deficient with respect to a theory of the media and the specificity of the gaze in each system of information machine/human interfaces. I shall here attempt to extend the Foucaultian analysis of the body and the surveilled subject by the addition of an exploration of the media, specifically cosmetic surgery reality TV.

There is another side of Foucault's work that is less prominent but perhaps even more germane to an understanding of reality TV than the analytics of power through surveillance and normativity. I refer to his later writings – *The History of Sexuality, Volumes 2 and 3*, and the Collège de France lectures of 1982 recently published in English as *The Hermeneutics of the Subject*. Foucault's concept of the care of self is most extensively developed in his book *The Hermeneutics of the Subject*, which ironically is taken from audio tapes of his lectures (with some corrections from his lecture notes). The medium of the audio cassette (as transposed into a printed book) is thus indispensable for an understanding of this central aspect of Foucault's late thinking on the relation of the self to the self or ethics. In these writings, along with the occasional pieces of the same years (interviews and lectures from 1980 to his death in 1984), Foucault initiates a second line of thought: not so much the analysis of the construction of the subject through technologies of power, conglomerations of discourse and practice, but the self-creation of the subject, his or her self-subjectivation, the complex ways the individual constitutes himself/herself through practices and enunciations. Foucault insists that his new project – a genealogy of ethics – is parallel to, while being distinct from, his earlier work:

> Three domains of genealogy are possible. First, a historical ontology of ourselves in relation to truth through which we constitute ourselves as subjects of knowledge; second, a historical ontology of ourselves in relation to a field of power through which we constitute ourselves as subjects acting on others; third, a historical ontology in relation to ethics through which we constitute ourselves as moral agents. (Foucault, 1997: 262)

The last project on self-subjectivation then does not supersede but rather complements the earlier work.

To be sure, in the late project on ethics, Foucault does not propose a new version of the liberal notion of the autonomous individual, self-reliant and free, one who builds a stable identity, like the comic character Baron von Munchausen, by lifting himself up by his own bootstraps. This Western conceit is after all the main subject of Foucault's critique and the chief preoccupation of his work. The poststructuralist in fact presents his notion of self-subjectivation as an alternative and overlooked or repressed stream of thinking in the West, one that has been overshadowed by the injunction "know thyself." Foucault formulates the tradition he points to as "the care of self," implying that this somewhat underground alternative culture might provide resources in the present for new types of emancipatory endeavors. Here he takes his cue from Nietzsche who foresaw a "transvaluation of values" in which ethics would be based not on renunciation and self-restraint but on aesthetics (Foucault, 1997: 262). Foucault anticipates the project of the hermeneutics of the subject contributing to a culture in which "everyone's life [might] become a work of art" (261). I shall raise the question of the care of self in relation to cosmetic surgery reality TV. Before embarking on this project, a thorough understanding is required of Foucault's idea of the care of self.

In the 1982 lectures at the Collège de France Foucault presented a genealogy of ethics in the Ancient World, concentrating on the Hellenistic period where "the care of self" reached its richest point of development. Foucault contrasts the care of self with the relation to the self in Platonism, Christianity, and modern philosophy, primarily Descartes. In all three cases, Foucault strives to distinguish the care of self as "spiritual" practices in which the self is transformed. In the care of self, the self is not discovered as it is in Descartes, or realized in its authenticity as it is in Sartre. Hellenistic care of self is a complex of life-long practices in which the individual attempts to change himself/herself. It is not a case in which the subject attempts to discover the truth of himself/herself, as in Plato, or to convert oneself in the image of a transcendent principle as in Christianity. Here is one definition Foucault gives of the Hellenistic care of the self:

One must live one's life in such a way that one cares for the self at
every moment and that at the enigmatic end of life . . . what one finds
. . . is precisely a certain relationship of self to self which is the crown,
realization, and reward of a life lived as test . . . One does not take care
of the self in order to live better or more rationally, and one does not
take care of the self in order to govern others properly . . . One must
live so as to establish the best possible relationship to oneself. (Foucault,
2005: 448)

The Greeks of the Hellenistic period developed a culture of self-
constitution, potentially open to all, through meditation, writing
exercises, group meetings and other practices. The direct goal was
an art of living, an aesthetic of self-relation, an ethic of spiritual
formation. This set of practices Foucault calls "care for the self"
included bodily exercise, relations with others, and observations of
the world. Yet its aim was a change in the mode of being of the self
(238).

Although the care of self emerged in Hellenistic times it was,
Foucault insists, "an event in thought" that "is still significant for
our modern mode of being subjects" (9). His intellectual history
thus has contemporary significance not in the possible replication
of the Hellenistic pattern of care of self but as a potential for adap-
tation in the current context. Foucault regrets the dominance of
Platonic, Christian, and Cartesian forms of relations of the subject
with truth, finding in the care of self a critical alternative. Indeed
he discerns a political aspect to the care of self. The care of self is,
he proclaims, "an urgent, fundamental and politically indispensable
task" (252). The relation one has with oneself is neither narcissism
nor self-indulgence but the "first or final point of resistance to
political power" (252). He connects the care of self with his more
obviously political projects:

. . . in the type of analysis I have been trying to advance for some time
you can see that power relations, governmentality, the government of
the self and of others, and the relationship of self to self constitute a
chain, a thread, and I think it is around these notions that we should
be able to connect together the question of politics and the question
of ethics. (252)

Care of self is thus a dimension of resistance, perhaps the basis of cultural contestation.

There is a tendency in cultural studies to conflate Foucault's notions of governmentality and care of self with neo liberal forms of domination and discipline. In this view, neoliberalism requires individuals to discipline themselves, especially as consumers and with the aid of the media, especially television (Hay, 2003: 165–206). Practices of consumption and media participation are here but one more vehicle through which the state ensures the smooth functioning of capitalism. The work one does on oneself folds into the prescriptions of the economy. The more one attempts to change one's mode of being, the more one supports the existing regime. While there is no doubt some truth to this line of argumentation, it closes the circle too quickly and too tightly. Anything one does might be interpreted as fitting into "neoliberalism." Protesting the war can be seen as proof that democracy works in America. If this line of interpretation is totalized, resistance becomes impossible and the impression is given that the social field is a homogenous landscape without gaps, openings, lines of flight. Acknowledging the danger that care of self might be just what the doctor orders for neoliberalism, I nonetheless shall focus on teasing out aspects of transgression and resistance in the phenomenon of cosmetic surgery reality TV.

One more aspect of Foucault's position must be clarified before I begin. As we have seen, Foucault rarely addresses the idea of the care of self in relation to contemporary culture. But one distinction about the care of self is crucial and must be borne in mind. In response to a question from Paul Rabinow and Hubert Dreyfus suggesting the common narcissism in modern society and ancient Greek ethics, Foucault offers the following comment: "In the Californian cult of the self, one is supposed to discover one's true self . . . not only do I not identify this ancient culture of the self with what you might call the Californian cult of the self, I think they are diametrically opposed" (Foucault, 1997: 271). If *I Want a Famous Face* and *The Swan* are understood only as depictions of individuals in quest for their true selves, then clearly the issue is not one that concerns Foucault's idea of the care of self. I want rather to inquire if there is a hint of care of self in these most abject television series.

For as Foucault writes, our culture, complex as it is, does not easily support this idea: "We have hardly any remnant of the idea in our society that the principal work of art which one must take care of, the main area to which one must apply aesthetic values, is oneself, one's life, one's existence" (Foucault, 1997: 271).

Surgeries reexamined

The question I shall pose in relation to *The Swan* and *I Want a Famous Face* is this: what can be learned about these shows when they are approached from the vantage point of the concept of the care of self? What does such an interrogation reveal about popular culture at a time when the media are disseminated throughout society ever more densely and with increasing variation and intermediation (Hayles, 2005)? Finally, what do the results of the analysis indicate about the heightened level of interaction between humans and information machines? I shall review aspects of the shows already discussed above but now analyze them through the lenses of the cultural theories of Foucault and Baudrillard.

During the second season of *I Want a Famous Face*, MTV aired a segment on May 24, 2005 in which Jamie, age 19 from Huntington Beach in the O.C., undergoes cosmetic surgery to make her look more like Posh Spice. Her second stated motive for the surgery is to impress her hairdresser, Steven, who she wants to be her boyfriend. Jamie complains that her nose is "heinous." Third, she hopes to become a hairstyle model. Like the contestants on *The Swan* and other participants in *I Want a Famous Face*, the surgery patients are self-critical about their physical appearance. The women in particular, especially on *The Swan*, regularly complain that in middle school they were teased relentlessly about their bodies, leaving a deep mark on their psyches and a strong sense of inadequacy. Of the 2 million "young people" announced as cosmetic surgery patients in 2003 by the voice-over on *I Want a Famous Face*, the vast majority, judging from the reality TV series, suffer from horrible self-images. One difference between the two shows is that on *The Swan* female contestants are presented initially without make-up, looking their worst, and announcing their psychic traumas and emotional suffering. On *I Want a Famous Face* subjects make good appearances from the outset and speak with confidence about wanting to improve their appearance. They have practical objectives in mind – furthering careers as models, for example.

The moral tone of *I Want a Famous Face* is muted. Reality here is about improving oneself through the single practice of cosmetic surgery. The only negative aspect of the presentation is that in the middle of every episode a counter example is presented. Another person's experience is reviewed in which the individual underwent a failed cosmetic surgery, some with serious medical consequences, others with little or no improvement in their desired physical appearance. It is unclear why the producers of *I Want a Famous Face* repeat this warning in every episode except perhaps for insurance purposes, in case viewers decide to copy the show and elect surgery with bad results. At another point in the show, a drawing of the patient's body appears on the screen, indicating the parts of the body to be cut and the cost for each surgery. One conceit of *I Want a Famous Face* is that the subject will pay for the surgery. Almost certainly MTV will foot the bill.

The Swan is quite different: a team of "experts" is assembled for the comprehensive transformation of the contestant. The group consists of two cosmetic surgeons, a dental surgeon, a psychologist, a physical trainer, and a dietician. A rigorous regime is imposed on the subject, covering all aspects of their mind and body. The contestant becomes a case in Foucault's sense, open to the medical gaze, scrutinized for signs of improvement or slippage. The subject is sequestered away from her home for several months, with no mirror, as the moderator emphasizes. The purpose of excluding mirrors from the patient's living quarters is to heighten the drama of "the reveal," when the individual sees themselves after the surgery for the first time. In the Jamie episode of *I Want a Famous Face*, by contrast, a cat is pictured briefly looking at itself in a mirror and seeing a lion. *The Swan* imposes a difficult trial on the contestant with extensive surgery performed on the body, long work-outs in the gym, and careful control of food intake. A total life conversion is at stake for the individual. Great rewards are offered from the show from the cost of the surgery to the promise of becoming the swan. *I Want a Famous Face* promises nothing, with benefits defined by the participant alone.

Both reality TV series are open to critique as means of disciplining the participants and the audience, subjecting them to heteronormative ideals of beauty, and medical technologies of power. On the episode of *The Swan* in which the winners of each week's competition participate in the final beauty pageant to select "the swan," observers note that the dozen or so contestants look very much like each other. They have similar hairdos, similar facial features, similar body shapes. Apparently the "objective" judgments of the team of medical experts impose similar images of beauty on all participants. Although contestants indicate to the experts their preferences for surgical operations, the doctors in most cases make the final decisions. What ORLAN self-consciously recognizes and deconstructs as models of beauty from Western art history, cosmetic surgeons on *The Swan* cut and stitch without awareness of imposing conformist norms.[6] Participants on *I Want a Famous Face* are more assertive in their prescriptions for surgery, selecting the celebrity of choice as a model, almost in the manner of ORLAN, insisting that the surgeons follow their wishes. Surgeons on *I Want a Famous Face*, it might be noted, are presented as cautious and "professional," warning their clients that they will not become clones of celebrities of their choice. On *The Swan* the doctors are authoritative in designing the surgeries. In both cases the selection of surgery already betrays the individual's acceptance of heteronormative images of beauty as they are defined by the culture industry and the doctor, a male in every case, still has influence over the outcome of the procedures.

Nevertheless on both TV series individuals engage in self-transformation, in an ethic of care for the self. For one thing they participate in transgressive television broadcasts in the sense of bringing "private" medical procedures into "public" media space. They reveal to the television audience aspects of their personal lives in a way that until recently was very rare in broadcast media. Both shows recognize that they are pushing the limits of acceptability, *I Want a Famous Face* by inserting a segment of a failed surgical procedure and *The Swan* by its posh, chateau-like setting, its homage to "the team of experts" and its Puritanical morality that judges contestants by how hard they worked to change themselves. These are defense mechanisms to gain audience acceptance for crossing the line of privacy. If Andrejevic is correct that televised self-confession is part of a new regime of neoliberal domination, it is also true that public display of personal life in cosmetic surgeries breaches the line of respectability as it existed in 2004. For ordinary people, without acting skills or training, to expose intimate acts to countless viewers is a performance that violates the rules learned in their upbringing and socialization. The surgeries may be interpreted as new modes of care of self both for the participants and for the audience. The shows validate and legitimize an ethic of self-transformation in an age of mediated culture, one certainly different from the case of the Hellenistic era discussed by Foucault but one perhaps more consonant with a time when information machines are in a new relation with humans.[7] From this perspective, the surgeries on reality TV might be seen as moves toward new forms of care of self that, while not liberatory or resistant in themselves, explore possibilities of subjectivation in the current formation of mediated culture.

Baudrillard's theory of the hyperreal becomes exigent at this point in the analysis.[8] Reality TV as exemplified in the cosmetic surgery series, as Murray and Ouelette argue, fascinates the audience because the subjects emerge on the screen out of everyday life. The viewers see people like themselves undergoing potentially life-changing surgeries and taking serious risks. What happens on the tube to the bodies of the participants happens in their extra-media life. The changes their bodies undergo remain after the broadcast, conserving an element of "reality" beyond the hyperreal. And yet reality is in question. What the audience experiences is mediated by the televisual apparatus. Viewers watch and listen to the emotional agony of the subjects and see close-ups of the actual operation. In a certain sense they witness the patient's ordeal more closely than friends and relatives, hence the hyperreal. At the same time, the broadcast is carefully staged, edited, and assembled, like any sitcom or police drama, even if there is no script. It is interrupted by advertisements and is strategically programmed by the network. It competes with shows on other networks and falls before and after programming that presumably enhances its chances of gleaning a large audience. It also becomes part of the larger media landscape of the Internet, the telephone network, newspapers, and magazines. In this sense, the cosmetic surgery series are media content. Their "reality" is actual enough but is different from non-media reality because, and this is my main argument, information machines are central to the human experience. These reality TV episodes are experienced with machines and further the construction of new configurations of human/information machine assemblages. Whatever impact the shows have on the viewers regarding their fascination with cosmetic surgery or with the selection of the swan must be understood also as the development of a culture of human/information machine apparatuses. I understand the hyperreal as a salient aspect of popular culture in the age of these interfaces. We are in the epoch of the posthuman (or postmodern, if you wish) where the determination of what is private and what is public is fundamentally configured by the role of information machines in everyday life. The intimacies beamed to the audiences of *The Swan* and *I Want a Famous Face* are conditioned by the new media landscape. How then are forms of the relation of the self to the self enabled and constructed in the media context? How does the care of self emerge here in constellations different from what was possible in Hellenistic culture and in modern culture?

Foucault's understanding of the care of self did not take media into consideration with the exception of practices of writing among the ancients. The cosmetic surgery reality TV shows, however, indicate a form of the care of self in which the media is crucial. Jamie undergoes surgeries in front of the camera, bringing her private life into the public sphere. Her care of self is enacted within televisual media. She changes herself to look more like Posh Spice, to attract the hairdresser, and to further her career all through the media performance. Television is changed (by airing private events), the audience is changed (by sharing these intimacies), and Jamie is changed first physically by the medical operations and also by her appearance on television. The private and the public are realigned through these shows forming a new constellation of mediated experience, of remote intimacy. The care of self now requires information machines for its fulfillment. All the self-revelations on the *Jerry Springer Show* and in blogs, podcasts, and websites bespeak the new formation. Information machines now provide the cultural space of the new public/private divide. Sharon Cumberland speaks of gender issues in the same terms: "Women are using the paradox of cyberspace – personal privacy in a public forum – to explore feelings and ideas that were considered risky or inappropriate for women in the past" (Cumberland, 2003: 275). These desires, she argues, enable women "to defy many of the social taboos that have inhibited self-exploration and self-expression" (ibid.). I would add or amend her proposition by changing "self-expression" to care of self. If there are new practices of the care of self they will be carried out mainly with the use of the Internet, television, telephones mobile and wired, handheld computers, and so forth.

Foucault raises the issue of conversion regarding the care of self, the degree to which practices that impinge on the relation of oneself to oneself result in a makeover, as it is called in reality TV, of the self. Foucault compares conversions among the Hellenistic Greeks and Romans, the Christians in the Middle Ages and the revolutionaries of 1789 and beyond. In the first case, conversion is a shift from an outward toward an inward set of practices, aiming to perfect the relation to oneself (Foucault, 2005: 210). It is less of an abrupt change than it would become later for Christians. It did not entail a renunciation of self or being reborn as it did among the Christians. What fascinates Foucault about conversion in the Hellenistic way of care for the self is the movement it incurs of turning away from the world and establishing and working on a relation to oneself. This is one of the "radical" aspects of the ancient care for the self, one that resonates in the contemporary era.

Participants on *The Swan* and *I Want a Famous Face* are clearly not turning away from the world, quite the opposite: they are making public aspects of their care for the self that in the modern period of bourgeois culture were regarded as private. This is the decisive turn that I regard as innovative: by bringing themselves into the public view, into the visibility of television, they also bring the mode of the care for the self directly into the mediated situation of contemporary culture. Information machines, in this case television and video recording devices, enter centrally into the equation of the care for the self. What had been hidden in modern media cultures like film now becomes available for all to see. What had been special to celebrities and the rich now becomes appropriate (if still not completely affordable) for everyone. Care for the self as mediated cosmetic surgery enters the general cultural domain and becomes a solicitation to everyone to consider, an interpellation of the audience not only as a specific practice of cutting the body but also as the serious question of the care for the self in general.

Conclusion

Obviously participants in both *The Swan* and *I Want a Famous Face* are deeply influenced by the heterosexual gender system. Although one participant on *I Want a Famous Face* was a transsexual, everyone else was heterosexual, sustaining the "regime of sexuality" as Foucault terms our current culture of desire. But as the participants on the shows carry out their project of reform they are engaging themselves in a transformation, they are undergoing changes that in part are spiritual or ethical in nature, they are forming new relations to themselves and making, despite appearances of subservience to culturally dominant norms, an art of living. If taking oneself seriously and caring for oneself in the twenty-first century requires, as in Jamie's case, operations to change the body, even with its dangers, then so be it. The surgeries broadcast to the nation are steps in the life of the participants that are at once disciplining and caring for the self, firmly bolting the body to the apparatuses of capitalism in its global stage and forming new relations with the self in the media space of television. The extreme makeover of cosmetic surgery does not conform to the Californian cult of identity as Foucault understands it, the always already center of the self that one must somehow discover or actualize, the true self at last. Instead participants in the shows alter themselves to mimic external standards either of celebrities or of the medical image of beauty. They change in unforeseen ways. They go down a road with no signposts and no predictable destination. They are not actualizing themselves, achieving their "true" identity, but exploring possibilities of personhood in the age of information machines.

Notes

1 I benefited greatly from comments and discussions of a draft of this chapter at a University of California Humanities Research Institute Seminar on "The Object of Media Studies." Participants in the discussion were Mary Desjardins, Raiford Guins, Amelie Hastie, Nguyen Tan Hoang, Laura Hyun Yi Kang, Kate Mondloch, Lisa Parks, and Mark Williams.

2 For an important collection on reality TV in general see Friedman (2002).

3 O'Leary (2002) argues that "*souci de soi*" is best translated as "care of self" to avoid making "self" into a substantive.

4 For a feminist analysis of *Extreme Makeover* that argues on lines similar to Andrejevic, see Weber (2005).

5 Baudrillard's first foray into reality TV is found in his relatively long comments on the public television documentary about the Loud family of Santa Barbara, California in 1971. Here he analyzes the show as a "verité experiment" seeing it as a "mechanism of surveillance" and as a simulacrum (Baudrillard, 1994: 27–32).

6 The role of cinema in promoting the culture of cosmetic surgery is analyzed by Vivian Sobchack with her usual intellectual dash in ch. 2, "Scary Women: Cinema, Surgery, and Special Effects," of Sobchack (2004).

7 Celia Lury brilliantly discusses such novelties as what she calls "prosthetic culture" and "experimental individualism" (Lury, 1998). I am leery about the term "prosthesis" since it suggests a human point of view as opposed to a perspective that registers the new subject position in relation to an interaction of humans with information machines. Lury does associate prosthetic culture with the medium of photography and with the general formation of images in mediated culture. To that degree my analysis of reality TV surgeries is in line with her argument. And she does use the idea of prosthesis not simply as additions to the self but also as transforming the self in the process. Yet I hesitate to frame the emergent mode of care of self as prosthetic.

8 Baudrillard's comments about plastic surgery are scattered throughout his writing. See for instance "Operation Whitewash," in Baudrillard (1993: 44–50).

References

Andrejevic, M. (2004) *Reality TV: The Work of Being Watched*. New York: Rowman & Littlefield Publishers.

Appadurai, A. (1996) *Modernity at Large: Cultural Dimensions of Globalization*. Minneapolis, MN: University of Minnesota Press.

Baudrillard, J. (1983) *Simulations*. New York: Semiotext(e).

Baudrillard, J. (1993) *The Transparency of Evil: Essays on Extreme Phenomena*. London and New York: Verso.

Baudrillard, J. (1994) *Simulacra and Simulation*. Ann Arbor, MI: University of Michigan Press.

Baudrillard, J. (2001) *Impossible Exchange*. New York: Verso.

Baudrillard, J. (2002) "Telemorphosis," in: *Ctrl [Space]*. T. Levin, U. Frohne and P. Weibel (eds). Cambridge, MA: MIT Press; 480–5.

Baudrillard, J. (2005) "The violence of the virtual and integral reality," *International Journal of Baudrillard Studies*, 2, 2.

Baym, N. K. (2000) *Tune In, Log On: Soaps, Fandom, and Online Community*. Thousand Oaks, CA: Sage.

Bolter, J. D. and Grusin, R. (1999) *Remediation: Understanding New Media*. Cambridge, MA: MIT Press.

Brecht, B. (1979–1980) "On Radio," *Screen*, 20, 3–4: 19.

Cumberland, S. (2003) "Private Uses of Cyberspace: Women, Desire, and Fan Culture," in: *Rethinking Media Change: The Aesthetics of Transition*. D. Thorburn and H. Jenkins (eds). Cambridge, MA: MIT Press; 261–79.

Enzensberger, H. M. (1982) "Constituents of a Theory of Media," in: *Critical Essays*. New York: Continuum.

Foucault, M. (1997) *Ethics: Subjectivity and Truth*. P. Rabinow (ed.). Trans. R. Hurley et al. New York: New Press.

Foucault, M. (2005) *The Hermeneutics of the Subject: Lectures at the Collège de France, 1981–1982*. New York: Palgrave.

Friedman, J. (ed.) (2002) *Reality Squared: Televisual Discourse on the Real*. New Brunswick, NJ: Rutgers University Press.

Hay, J. (2003) "Unaided Virtues: The (Neo)Liberalization of the Domestic Sphere and the New Architecture of Community," in: *Foucault, Cultural Studies, and Governmentality*. J. Bratich, J. Packer and C. McCarthy (eds). Albany, NY: SUNY Press; 165–206.

Hayles, K. (2005) *My Mother Was a Computer: Digital Subjects and Literary Texts*. Chicago, IL: University of Chicago Press.

Jones, A. (1998) *Body Art/Performing the Subject*. Minneapolis, MN: University of Minnesota Press.

Lury, C. (1998) *Prosthetic Culture: Photography, Memory and Identity*. New York: Routledge.

McCarthy, A. (2001) *Ambient Television: Visual Culture and Public Space*. Durham, NC: Duke University Press.

McLuhan, M. (1964) *Understanding Media: The Extensions of Man*. New York: McGraw-Hill.

Murray, S. and Ouellette, L. (2004) "Introduction," in: *Reality TV: Remaking Television Culture*. S. Murray and L. Ouellette (eds). New York: University Press; 1–15.

O'Bryan, J. (2004) *Carnal Art: ORLAN's Refacing*. Minneapolis, MN: University of Minnesota Press.

O'Leary, T. (2002) *Foucault and the Art of Ethics*. New York: Continuum.

Poster, M. (1995) *The Second Media Age*. Cambridge, MA: Blackwell.

Sobchack, V. (2004) *Carnal Thoughts: Embodiment and Moving Image Culture*. Berkeley, CA: University of California Press.

Spigel, L. (1992) *Make Room for TV: Television and the Family Ideal in Postwar America*. Chicago, IL: University of Chicago Press.

Weber, B. (2005) "Beauty, desire and anxiety: the economy of sameness in ABC's *Extreme Makeover*," *Genders Online Journal*, 41 (Spring).

Wills, D. (1995) *Prosthesis*. Stanford, CA: Stanford University Press.

5

Et in Arizona Ego: Baudrillard on the Planet of the Apes

John Beck

Reflecting on the prospects faced by his band of settlers as they disembarked from the *Mayflower* in the winter of 1620, William Bradford, writing some ten years after the event, positions the colonists as caught between an irretrievable past and an awful future. In front of them, all they can see is a "hideous and desolate wilderness, full of wild beasts and wild men." There is no turning back, for behind them "there was the mighty ocean which they had passed and was now as a main bar and gulf to separate them from all the civil parts of the world" (Bradford, 2002: 315–16). Apprehension of the New World is predicated here on the loss of any hope for a return to civilization. A similar sense of abandonment is experienced over three hundred and fifty years after Bradford's landfall by Jean Baudrillard, who claims that to "see and feel America . . . you have to have had for at least one moment . . . the feeling that Europe had disappeared" (Baudrillard, 1988: 104–5).

Physically and culturally bereft of context, Bradford and Baudrillard proceed to account for their presence in this cognitive wilderness by translating their experience into something they can understand. For Bradford this involves deploying the technology of Biblical exegesis known as typology, whereby scriptural antitypes can be interpreted as prefiguring persons, events, or places. Like the Israelites, the Puritans had escaped persecution and were now embarked on their "errand in the wilderness" to found the New Jerusalem. Despite its desolation, then, America is nevertheless soon recognizable to Bradford. Baudrillard, likewise, has a set of correspondences and analogies available that provide a means of gaining a footing in the New World: a stockpile of European notions about the US and a lifetime of watching American films and TV shows. Despite their disconsolate remarks about being unmoored from Europe, in each case America is approached, in the end, as something strangely familiar.

Since at least the publication of Mexican historian Edmundo O'Gorman's *El proceso de la invención de América* in 1958, it has become commonplace to observe that America was invented rather than discovered, and that invention preceded and defined the conditions of possibility through which any actual encounter with the continent could occur (O'Gorman, 1961). In the same year that the English translation of O'Gorman's study was published, influential British Americanist Marcus Cunliffe, writing in the literary journal *Encounter*, reiterated the point that for most Europeans "America has never existed" and only ever functioned as a myth (Cunliffe, 1991: 311). While the terminology, thanks in no small part to O'Gorman, has changed over the years, with contemporary historians drawing on discourses of "encounter" and "contact" between indigenous and explorer cultures rather than unidirectional narratives of "discovery" and "conquest" (Castillo, 2005; Pratt, 1992), the notion of an "imagined America" remains an influential model of how the US was made out of European fantasies of an unknown continent, whether these were religious hopes for an uncontaminated new beginning, enlightenment dreams of democracy, or the adventurer's longing for unimaginable wealth.

Baudrillard's 1986 book *America* is situated quite squarely within the substantial canon of works by Europeans about America that subscribe to one version or another of the "imagined America" model (Mathy, 1993). "France is just a country; America is a concept," Baudrillard reminded a *New York Times* interviewer in 2005 (Solomon, 2005), but it is a concept in material form, a kind of embodiment of ideas that have preceded it: "All of the themes that I first examined in my previous books suddenly appeared, in America, stretching before me in concrete form," he claimed in 1986 (Gane, 1993: 135). "I was here in my imagination," Baudrillard admits in *America*, "long before I actually came here" (Baudrillard, 1988: 72).

Like works from de Tocqueville to Henry James and beyond, Baudrillard constructs a binary relation between Europe and the US that allows him to make a series of quite familiar remarks about differences of time and space, nature and culture, barbarism and civilization, surface and depth. Students of Euro-American literature will recognize this strategy immediately, although it is not one confined to European writers; American literature also has its own inventory of "imagined Europes" (Bradbury, 1996; Giles, 2002). Conventionally, the alleged American propensity for geography over history, the unadorned over the elaborate, innocence over experience, action over reflection, is read as simultaneously invigorating and panic-inducing. These generalities are intended to register the extent to which America has liberated itself from hidebound tradition and prejudice but also the degree to which the future (America is always the future) will be infinitely more vulgar and shallow than the past. It is a measure of quite how steeped in transatlantic lore Baudrillard is that his writings on the US do all these things, and this is one of the main reasons the critical reception of *America* has been predominantly hostile. Conventional binaries come thick and fast in *America* and there is little sense that Baudrillard is ironically flirting with clichés. Rather, he appears to be lazily repeating them.

It is Baudrillard's status as a highly visible representative of something called French Theory that has no doubt produced so much criticism of *America*. Certainly, as I have already suggested, Baudrillard's book seems to be saying nothing that many other books about the US have been saying for two centuries. But the apparent laziness of Baudrillard's musings on the American character and the unreflective ease with which stereotypes are aired has often been used to cut a swathe through the philosophical high ground of wilfully opaque "postmodernists." The following example, from anthropologists Anna Grimshaw and Keith Hart, is fairly typical of the criticism Baudrillard has continued to receive: "As a representative example of much postmodernist writing in recent years, Baudrillard's *America* is an indictment of that whole intellectual class whose postwar prosperity has insulated them from the movement of modern history, so that they can only see in America a mirror reflecting their own alienation." Baudrillard, they claim, "thinks alone in a universe unmediated by the presence of others" (Grimshaw and Hart, 1990).

If we were looking for lazy repetitions of unreflective prejudice there are plenty here, including the suggestion that "postmodernist writing" represents little more than the self-indulgence of a privileged and out of touch, over-educated elite. There are far better and more convincing criticisms of Baudrillard's *America* than Grimshaw and Hart are able to muster in studies by, for example, Douglas Kellner (1990), Barry Smart (1993), and Caren Kaplan (1996), but my purpose here is less to rehearse these arguments again than to explore the possibility that there is more to Baudrillard's "imagined America" than the familiar prejudices of the European intellectual elite.

The fact is that the "imagined America" model is not merely an overdetermined Eurocentric narrative of discovery or invention but a profoundly powerful aspect of American political self-representation, bound up with the notion of "pursuit": the pursuit of liberty and happiness. Within this future-oriented libertarian quest-narrative, everything in America comes to signify the "idea" of America in just the way that Baudrillard envisions: American objects *are* American values. The collapse of metaphor that Europeans "grieve over" is, for Baudrillard, in America greeted with joy since this is a country where "things, faces, skies, and deserts are expected to be simply what they are" (Baudrillard, 1988: 27–8). So, in *America*, in order to approximate this "opportunity to be brutally naive," the banalities of US self-description are blithely reiterated: the blank sheet of the desert is waiting to be written upon; racial heterogeneity is evidence of emerging new identities; the conquest of space through acceleration is evidence of the speed by which objectives become fulfilled; what Baudrillard calls the "primitive" society of America – also referred to as "primeval" and "raw" – is guileless and therefore unencumbered, unrepressed, and "free" to pursue its desires. Cars, roads, motels, swimming pools, skyscrapers, soft drinks, plains, mountains, subways are never just things but incarnations of a self-presencing ideology: it is "a miracle of total availability" (1988: 8). Yes, this is a typical European reading of American material culture but it is also the common currency of the official narrative of American life as it is told by the institutions of government and commerce.

What Baudrillard is especially good at is showing what it is like to be alien to this discourse of America while having internalized all its rhetorical moves. Indeed, for Baudrillard there is no access to America outside the discourse of America: "What you have to do is enter the fiction of America, enter America as fiction." It is, he admits, "on this fictive basis that it dominates the world" (1988: 29). It is this suggestion of domination running through Baudrillard's account of his travels in the US that inflects even his most hyperbolic celebrations of Americana with a latent critical edge. "America is powerful and original," he writes, but it is also "violent and abominable. We should not seek to deny either of these aspects, nor reconcile them" (1988: 88).

The immense appeal of American popular culture and the pervasiveness of its global influence are not lost on Baudrillard, who is as enraptured by the material confirmation of treasured cinematic memories as any casual tourist to New York or Monument Valley. The kind of *unheimlich* experience Baudrillard registers in his book will not be unfamiliar to non-Americans visiting the US. This is because on-the-ground America is both the same as but also immeasurably different from the idea of America constructed out of its representational exports. As image repertoire the US is easily domesticated but as an inhabited place it is ferociously unruly. It is this, I think, that makes Baudrillard's *America* a revealing book: it speaks in a language – the American language of incarnational freedom – that it does not fully understand, like a kind of phonetic translation. Or, perhaps more accurately, it speaks a language that has been learned through reading and watching rather than through conversation. And it can do nothing but that since Baudrillard's point throughout his work on simulation is that there is no outside, no perspective from which the legitimizing rhetoric of American objects can be seen as rhetoric. It is in this respect that

America "dominates the world" and, for the first three-quarters of *America*, dominates Baudrillard's prose also.

A similar foreclosure of alternative perspectives can be seen in photographs taken in the US by Europeans such as German film-maker Wim Wenders or British photographer Michael Ormerod. In each case, their images replicate formally and in subject matter the work of generations of American photographers, as if the syntax of American visual culture resists different configurations and must always in the end say the same thing (Ormerod, 1994; Wenders, 2001). As with Baudrillard's writing on America, we must ask: are these works intentionally mimicking other works in some kind of homage? Are they ironically replaying familiar tropes for critical effect? Is it lack of imagination, narrowness of vision? Or is it that there is no outside to that way of looking, writing, representing? For Baudrillard, at least, I think the answer is the latter.

From inside the discourse of "imagined America" the traces of casual racism and sexism in Baudrillard's text are to be expected; from within the exceptionalist rhetoric of the capitalist–democratic world order, why shouldn't history be over? And from inside the lexicon of rugged individualism, why shouldn't Baudrillard "think alone in a universe unmediated by the presence of others"? This, surely, is the other side of American libertarianism – the right to be left alone to call the world into being in one's own image. From this point of view, Baudrillard comes across less like de Tocqueville and more like Daniel Boone, who had to keep moving west to get away from the communities he had made the country safe for. Closer still, Baudrillard resembles Charlton Heston's Taylor in *Planet of the Apes* (1968), a man hurled into an alien desert inhab-ited by the primitive civilization of the future – he is, he says, the "Aeronautic missionary of the silent majorities" (Baudrillard, 1988: 13). Certainly, some of Taylor's observations are not without the kind of hyperbole favored by Baudrillard: "time's wiped out eve-rything you ever knew – it's all dust"; "There is only one reality left. We are here and it is now"; "seen from out here everything seems different. Time bends, space is boundless. It squashes a man's ego. I feel lonely."

The *Planet of the Apes* analogy seems especially pertinent somehow. In the film, ape society is organized along tacitly democratic lines, but social order is maintained by the withholding of the truth of history – that human civilization preceded ape civilization – by the ruling caste of orangutans, who are holding on to power in the face of a volatile and dim but strong warrior class of gorillas. Liberal intellectual chimpanzees are powerlessly caught between the two and merely complain in private. Taylor is literally the last man, a throwback to a dead civilization whose values have, of course, produced the catastrophe that led to ape civilization in the first place. Unable to believe in a species greater than man, his resistance finally exposes the truth the apes have repressed: the apocalypse has already happened and the desert is in fact the remains of New York City. The famous closing scene of the film, with Taylor confronted by the ruins of the Statue of Liberty, is not only shocking as an image of America in ruins, but also is doubly destabilizing since it geographically throws us back to the East coast. From the beginning of the film, the visual environment has been a predominantly Western one. Taylor's spaceship crashes into Lake Powell near Page, Arizona, and the early part of the film draws on classic Western desert mis-en-scène. The cliffs at the end of the film are also part of a recognizably Western geography, this time the Southern Californian coastline around Malibu. When the crown of Liberty comes into view, the shock is partly achieved by the disorienting effect of having the quintessential icon of New York City planted in what is clearly a Pacific environment. As the arid Western landscape makes time visible, the film's climactic punch is achieved through an inversion of American geography. The West functions in the film as a vision of the post-catastrophe East: after the apocalypse, New York will look like Arizona and California – the East will look like the West *already* looks: blasted, inhospitable, and inhabited by the grotesque after-effects of a horrible but unfathomable history.

This is the kind of narrative Baudrillard constructs about the experience of being in America, where the West stands in for the whole of the US and, indeed, the world. Baudrillard is the last man, self-positioned as outside the society he has "discovered." What has come true for Taylor is that the monstrous other world he believes he has been arbitrarily flung into is in fact the product of his own world and his values: he is not lost but has been at home all along. "It is the American way of life," Baudrillard argues, a way of life Europeans think is "naive or culturally worthless," that will in fact offer a "graphic representation of the end of our values" (Baudrillard, 1988: 98). The horror in *America* is that Baudrillard, like Taylor in *Planet of the Apes*, discovers that he speaks the same language as the awful future society he has encountered.

America, J. Hoberman noted in a review of the English translation of the book, enshrines Baudrillard as "the poet laureate of Reagan's reign" (Hoberman, 1988: 15). In retrospect, this assessment is both true and false. *America* was published in the US just as the American love affair with Baudrillard – most ardently located in his seduction of the New York art world – was cooling off. Since the publication of *Simulations* by Semiotext(e) in 1983, Baudrillard's work had provided a fashionable "theoretical" articulation for the kind of neoconceptualist work being produced by artists such as Jeff Koons and Sherrie Levine. At a lecture at the Whitney Museum of Modern Art in 1987, however, Baudrillard repudiated his followers by claiming that they had entirely misunderstood his work. While Baudrillard's work had, as Sylvère Lotringer observes, "unwillingly contributed to reestablish the preeminence of sleek American art and even sleeker art market" after a period of European neoexpressionist dominance (Lotringer, 2001: 153), Baudrillard's refusal of the art world's embrace suggests a consistency in his critical assessment of simulation as the condition of advanced capitalism that is too easily misconstrued as acquiescence. To call Baudrillard the poet laureate of the Reagan era, then, is true inasmuch as Baudrillard's writing successfully moves inside the discourse of an emerging neoliberal American empire of simulated incarnational "American" values. But it is false in that Baudrillard's texts, especially his writing on America itself, perform their own absorption into those values with such troubling seamlessness that the absence of critical distance – the necessary condition with which the voiding of distance can be felt to have been voided – can easily be read as a refusal of criticism, rather than the enforced paralysis of criticism I think Baudrillard is seeking to represent.

Part of the power of *Planet of the Apes* as an allegory of America's moral malaise in the 1960s is that it presents Charlton Heston, the actor who had previously embodied the heroic Hollywood version of righteous, biblically proportioned American manhood in his roles as Ben Hur, John the Baptist, and Moses, not as the savior of mankind but as representative of the problem. The deflation of Heston-as-icon in *Planet of the Apes* and in subsequent apocalyptic survivalist films like *The Omega Man* (1971) and *Soylent Green* (1973) might be seen as the canny career move of a big league player who can sense the tide turning against him as the certainties of Cold War consensus culture are swept away by Vietnam-era paranoia. What is striking in *Planet of the Apes*, though, is that Taylor's cynicism and misanthropy at the start of the film do not merely suggest a thwarted romantic whose fears are realized by the film's climax, but these qualities are also positioned as intrinsic to the arrogance of the discourse of America's utopian incarnational virtue that is literally brought down to earth by the revelation of Liberty's ruins.

For Baudrillard, faced, like William Bradford and Taylor, with an apparently unsurpassable gulf between past and present, Old World and New World, prospects for the future yield only a "hideous and desolate wilderness, full of wild beasts and wild men," a kind of future anterior, a what-will-have-been. Bradford's solution is to read that wilderness as the ground upon which to prepare for Judgment Day. For Taylor, that day has long passed and he is forced to live "after history." What is "primitive" about the Reaganite America of the 1980s Baudrillard experiences is precisely the way the accretions of civil society brought about by public spending and legal protections since the New Deal have been so effectively dismantled through an appeal to a "primeval" conception of American individualism crafted out of the sum of its simulations and underpinned by an eschatological faith in a divine intervention that will ultimately provide an escape route from the depredations of a fallen world.

In fact, though Baudrillard appears to spend a good deal of *America* in thrall to the immense power of America as simulation, the final quarter of the book, especially in the passages on the Reagan presidency, deals directly with the implications of America's so-called "achieved utopia" with an incisiveness that throws the preceding pages into sharp relief. The sense of domination that sucks the air out of the book's more ecstatic moments is here, in its scrutiny of the Reagan regime, made explicit. It is Reagan, argues Baudrillard, who has attempted to convert the whole of America into a version of California (a "sunny screen memory"), introducing a system "where the easy life exerts a kind of blackmail, reviving the original American pact of an achieved utopia" (Baudrillard, 1988: 108). While individualism has survived from the original promise of democracy, the Reagan program has not preserved for Americans "a sense of meaning that could be collectively given to their undertakings" (1988: 108).

The consequence of Reagan's "triumphal illusionism" (1988: 108) is, Baudrillard speculates, that actuality has become indistinguishable from image, and the simulation of achieved utopia enables the erasure of inconvenient anomalies:

> But this easy life knows no pity. Its logic is a pitiless one. If utopia has already been achieved, then unhappiness does not exist, the poor are no longer credible. If America is resuscitated, then the massacre of the Indians did not happen, Vietnam did not happen. While frequenting the rich ranchers or manufacturers of the West, Reagan has never had the faintest inkling of the poor and their existence, nor the slightest contact with them. He knows only the self-evidence of wealth, the tautology of power, which he magnifies to the dimensions of the nation, or indeed of the whole world. The have-nots will be condemned to oblivion, to abandonment, to disappearance pure and simple. (1988: 111)

Here Baudrillard addresses the political economy of simulation with a directness that feeds back to critically reveal the rhetorical strategy of his own preceding text. There is no outside to the discourse of the "imagined America" because it is a function of American power to foreclose on alternatives and write them out of the script. The radical appropriation of the "achieved utopia narrative" by the Reaganite New Right means that the state's job to ensure social justice and protection "has now fallen within the scope of providential (presidential) decree. It is as though the Last Judgment had already happened. The good have been found virtuous, the others have been cast out. No need for good will any more. No need to feel guilty" (1988: 112).

What Baudrillard identifies in Reagan is the beginnings of the process of neoliberal restructuring that, over the next twenty years, will reshape the biopolitical relationship between the citizen and the state. Here Baudrillard begins to sound distinctly Foucauldian in his reflections on exclusionary practices that anticipate the political debates of the early twenty-first century:

> The policies of governments are themselves becoming negative. They are no longer designed to socialize, to integrate, or to create new rights. Behind the appearance of socialization and participation they are desocializing, disenfranchising, and dejecting. The social order is contracting to include only economic exchange, technology, the sophisticated and innovative; as it intensifies these sectors, entire zones are "disintensified," becoming reservations, and sometimes not even that: dumping grounds, wastelands, new deserts for the new poor, like the deserts you see forming around nuclear power stations or motor-ways. Nothing will be done to save them and perhaps nothing can be done, since enfranchisement, emancipation, and expansion have already taken place. (1988: 113)

Toward the end of *America*, then, Baudrillard is beginning to sketch out a broad understanding of the function of simulation as a means of sustaining and extending political power at home and American dominance overseas. Faced with the end of the Cold War, America is "suffering from the disappearance of ideologies that might contest its power and from the weakening of all the forces that previously opposed it" (1988: 115). As "uncontested, uncontestable," American power is now, for Baudrillard, "a model (business, the market, free enterprise, performance) – and a universal one – even reaching as far as China. The international style is now American" (1988: 116). The effect is, he argues, that the absence of meaningful enemies means that the US can take credit for victory without having done anything. The stability resulting from this phoney victory is fragile, "a potential stabilization by inertia, of an assumption of power in a vacuum" (1988: 116).

In *America* there is no outside of the American rhetoric of achieved utopia; for Baudrillard, it erases all alternatives. While Reagan's revived Cold War was driven by an ascendant New

Right that reinstated American exceptionalism and the unquestionable legitimacy of God's chosen people to fight externalized "evil," at least the target was a moribund Soviet Union. It was Reagan's spending power, appropriately, that in the end helped bring down the Russians. While the Bush II regime has sought to appeal to the same reified American values of freedom – advice to New Yorkers post-9/11: go shopping – the fact is that the enemy cannot be so conveniently externalized. Here, I think, Baudrillard's 1980s recognition of there being no outside of America's global syntax of achieved utopian power takes on new significance.

In *The Spirit of Terrorism* (2002), Baudrillard recognizes that the 9/11 attacks indicate that the very dominance of the American system has made possible the circumstances for violent resistance:

> When global power monopolises the situation to this extent, when there is such formidable condensation of all functions in the technocratic machinery, and when no alternative form of thinking is allowed, what other way is there but a *terroristic situational* transfer? It was the system itself which created the objective conditions for the brutal retaliation. (Baudrillard, 2002: 8–9)

Here there is an enemy "which plays the game, solely with the aim of disrupting it," who "have taken over all the weapons of the dominant power. Money and stock-market speculation, computer technology and aeronautics, spectacle and media networks – they have assimilated everything of modernity and globalism, without changing their goal, which is to destroy that power" (2002: 19). This last observation is the key, I think, since it refutes the notion of American discourse as a totalizing fiction and suggests that its syntax can be worked to say different things. The fact is that the enemy have "used the banality of American everyday life as cover or camouflage" (2002: 9).

At this point Baudrillard asks us to do something he previously found impossible to do with regard to the US: to think outside the constraints of the dominant model. We must, he argues, "slough off our Western perspective" (2002: 21). This is true, and the Bush regime's inability (and unwillingness) to do so has been catastrophic. But it is not clear how this is to be achieved. In order

to describe America in the 1980s Baudrillard found himself simulating American clichés of time and space. Then, the preposition
"we" referred to Europeans; "they" were Americans, even as his
narrative mimicked the dominant American discourse of achieved
utopia. In *The Spirit of Terrorism*, the "we" refers to Westerners,
"they" are the "enemy." While Baudrillard suggests "we" are to
think like "them," he is still, it seems, inclined to work in terms of
binaries not dissimilar to those utilized by official American (and
British) discourse determined to externalize the other side.

What the 9/11 attacks revealed for Baudrillard, however, is that
there is another side, a reading of American power that can move
inside it but remains other to it. The unknowable nature of this
other side is captured quite accurately by Baudrillard's deployment
of the "us" and "them" binary: what is baffling for "us" is that
"they" have become rich "without ceasing to wish to destroy us"
(2002: 23). Flying in the face of all we know about the accumulation
of wealth as coterminous with the fortification of state power, "the
new rules are not ours to determine" (2002: 23). The indecipher-
ability of this new lexicon can, Baudrillard argues, only partially and
inaccurately be translated back into the American (now Western
or globalized capitalist) discourse of incarnational righteousness:
"our" explanations for terrorism fail to comprehend that which is
beyond it (2002: 23–6). At the same time, the effectiveness of that
discourse, through its "uninterrupted profusion of banal images and
a seamless flow of sham events" – precisely the effect produced in
America – has been punctured by the radicalization of images and
events as deployed and reimagined by the terrorists (2002: 27).

The "idea of freedom," Baudrillard surmises, "is already fading
from minds and mores"; global deregulation "ends up in a
maximum of constraints and restrictions" (2002: 32). Reading
America through *The Spirit of Terrorism*, it becomes clear that this
has always been the point of Baudrillard's thinking on the US. The
claustrophobic banality of the earlier book, so often criticized at
the time as the lazy repetition of clichés, might now be understood
more properly as the articulation of the prison-house of American
discourse from which Baudrillard felt, then, there was no escape.
His refusal to endorse the New York art world's reading of his
work because such a reading merely furthered the affirmative

nature of the art market trading on his name indicates a knowing-
ness that the publication of *America* in English in 1988 confirms. In
his review for the *Voice Literary Supplement*, Hoberman notes that
America has appeared "just as the author seems poised to pass from
intellectual fashion" (Hoberman, 1988: 15). Since he was already
aware of the art world's misreading of his work, *America* could be
said to function in part as an act of sabotage, at once a supercharged
confirmation of everything misunderstood about Baudrillard-as-
celebrity and an incapacitating repetition of the very values and
tropes his American readership had previously relied upon him to
critically transvalue. Read this way, *America* becomes a toxic gift to
America of its own self-image as refracted through the enervated
gaze of the European intellectual class. At the same time, *America*
offers a lacerating reading of American simulation as a function
of American hegemony that not only skewers the yuppies (busy
investing in the New York art market critically buoyed up by its
flirtation with Baudrillard) but also sketches out the contours of
post-Cold War American biopolitical ambitions.

As his observations in *The Spirit of Terrorism* suggest, the gap
opened up in America's global dominance by the 9/11 attacks
is read by Baudrillard as something of an opportunity through
which his own imagining of an outside can be pursued. In the
later book, Baudrillard's willingness to include himself among
the "we" is deployed to articulate "our" bewildered state in the
face of a genuine Rumsfeldian "unknown unknown." Failure to
conceive of life outside the incarnational discourse of an "imagined America" has generated the catastrophe always implicit in the
eschatological tendencies it inherited from Reagan. Post-9/11,
America seems remarkably alive to the dangers of an "uncontested,
uncontestable" American superpower. The inability of the book
to move beyond the lexicon of American discursive self-imagining
now seems like less of a failure on Baudrillard's part and more of an
indictment of the hold that discourse had over American cultural
and political life, a hold that extended to include non-Americans'
capacity to apprehend the US as anything but what it said it was.
The Europe that Baudrillard felt had "disappeared" in America may
be irretrievable but the incantations of an "imagined America" are
no longer enough.

References

Baudrillard, Jean (1988) *America*. Trans. Chris Turner. London: Verso.

Baudrillard, Jean (2002) *The Spirit of Terrorism* Trans. Chris Turner. London: Verso.

Bradbury, Malcolm (1996) *Dangerous Pilgrimages: Transatlantic Mythologies and the Novel*. New York: Viking.

Bradford, William (2002) "Of Plymouth Plantation," in: Paul Lauter (ed.) *The Heath Anthology of American Literature*. Volume 1, 4th edition. pp. 313–34. Boston, MA: Houghton Mifflin.

Castillo, Susan (2005) *Colonial Encounters in New World Writing, 1500–1786: Performing America*. New York: Routledge.

Cunliffe, Marcus (1991) "European Images of America," in: *In Search of America: Transatlantic Essays, 1951–1990*. pp. 309–31. New York: Greenwood.

Gane, Mike (ed.) (1993) *Baudrillard Live: Selected Interviews*. New York: Routledge.

Giles, Paul. (2002) *Virtual Americas: Transnational Fictions and the Transatlantic Imaginary*. Durham, NC: Duke University Press.

Grimshaw, Anna, and Hart, Keith (1990) "James, de Tocqueville and Baudrillard." The C.L.R. James Institute (http://www.clrjamesinstitute. org/baudrill.html)

Hoberman, J. (1988) "Lost in America: Jean Baudrillard, Extraterrestrial," *Voice Literary Supplement*, March, pp. 15–16.

Kaplan, Caren (1996) *Questions of Travel: Postmodern Discourses of Displacement*. Durham, NC: Duke University Press.

Kellner, Douglas (1990) *Jean Baudrillard: From Marxism to Postmodernism and Beyond*. Stanford, CA: Stanford University Press.

Lotringer, Sylvère (2001) "Doing Theory," in Sylvère Lotringer and Sande Cohen (eds), *French Theory in America*. pp. 125–162. New York: Routledge.

Mathy, Jean-Philippe (1993) *Extrême-Occident: French Intellectuals and America*. Chicago, IL: University of Chicago Press.

O'Gorman, Edmundo (1961) *The Invention of America: An Inquiry into the Historical Nature of the New World and the Meaning of Its History*. Bloomington, IN: University of Indiana Press.

Ormerod, Michael (1994) *States of America*. Manchester, UK: Cornerhouse.

Pratt, Mary Louise (1992) *Imperial Eyes: Studies in Travel Writing and Transculturation*. New York: Routledge.

Smart, Barry (1993) "Europe/America," in: Chris Rojek and Bryan S. Turner (eds), *Forget Baudrillard?* pp. 47–69. New York: Routledge.

Solomon, Deborah (2005) "Continental Drift," *New York Times Magazine*. November 20. (http://www.nytimes.com/2005/11/20/magazine/20wwln_q4.html)

Wenders, Wim (2001) *Written in the West*. Kempen, Germany: teNeues.

6

Pursuit in Paris

John Armitage

Two o'clock in the hot afternoon in Paris on Wednesday, August 1, 2007, and we didn't feel like doing very much.[1] Yet, lounging in our room (chambre 47) at the Hôtel Raspail-Montparnasse ("Charme & confort dans un style Art-déco"), a bizarre curiosity encouraged us to visit the grave in Cimetière Montparnasse of Jean Baudrillard, the celebrated French cultural theorist who died on March 6, 2007. Enthused by a desire to contemplate the mysteries of Baudrillard's cultural theory and to be close to him, we also wanted to ask what death has done to Baudrillard, to contemporary cultural theory, and to visual culture? We said to ourselves, "Where is that mischievous high priest of postmodernism now who wielded so much theoretical power and cultural influence, where is his notorious impact on the contemporary visual and social scene, on our own and others' lives?"

We started by hunting haphazardly for the signs to Cimetière Montparnasse, at the point where Boulevard Montparnasse meets Boulevard Raspail.

We were continuing with the captivating idea that both the signs to Cimetière Montparnasse and our own summer vacation were part of a random dérive, a form, a practice of experimental urban and cultural behavior, lacking preconceived meaning, and

advancing, psychologically and geographically speaking, purely through fleeting, atmospheric, and indeterminate passageways.

However, we did not sense that our lives would be incomplete if we did not manage to find Baudrillard's tomb. In any case, he did not know us and we did not really know him. To some extent, then, we were following something both within and beyond ourselves without, at least initially, knowing what it was. Were we really executing this dérive in order to locate Baudrillard's grave? Or were we looking for something beyond the tomb of the unknown and almost certainly unknowable cultural soldier?

Alternatively, and perhaps more likely, we were responding to what the American continental philosopher and traveler Alphonso Lingis (1998) calls the imperatives in things. Lingis, of course, has radically transformed the style and substance of contemporary Western philosophy. Widely admired as a unique and significant thinker, translator of Emmanuel Levinas (1969) and Maurice Merleau-Ponty (1968), his writings are at once closely argued, sensual, illustrated with photographs, and offer works of extraordinarily suggestive force. Encompassing philosophy, anthropology, and travelog, Lingis's oeuvre investigates everything from Japanese literature (Yukio Mishima) and psychoanalysis (Jacques Lacan) to the key figures of Western continental philosophy such as Martin Heidegger and Michel Foucault. Resisting the artificial boundaries between the body and subjectivity, his writings comprise a completely remodeled phenomenology of the self, the other, and the world. For beneath the landscape of things on which our adventures unfold, Lingis proposes, there is also submersion in the elements, in the radiance of the environment, in the sonority of the heat of the day, and in the support of the earth. Pleasure, sensuality, and bodily movement, then, are all responses to the sensory elements and to the levels, to how intimate and alien things take shape, to things as important and as part of rational action, but which only secondarily interlock with the passageways and the production of our purposeful world. Consequently, the elements, the levels, the spectacle of things, and the ends that order our environment serve not so much as directives as imperatives:

> The imperatives in things, the imperatives things are, do not order us with an imperative for a universal and necessary form of response our thought would program for our sensibility; they order the diagrams and variations of our postural schema and exploratory manipulations. A thing is there not as a given and not as a possibility or a hypothesis but as an imperative. (Lingis, 1998: 64)

Here, to see things has nothing whatever to do with Baudrillard's (1991) concept of seduction or with presenting oneself as another's reflection. Rather, it has everything to do with observing how we have to remain and to move toward things, to explore them, and to perceive what they and we need to survive. It was therefore not a matter of our becoming, of tracing Baudrillard's final destination, or of trying to replicate his biographical narrative or intellectual dérive, the latter of which, to be sure, had many connotations for him. Instead, it was a matter of seeing how the fragile meanings of his cultural theory can and have to be not so much copied as conserved, sheltered, restored, and, crucially, developed. It was as though people beyond Baudrillard had to understand how his theories of culture and conceptions of visuality can and have to be preserved, investigated, and expanded if they are to be advanced in the future. Baudrillard's indefinable objectives, we said, were now our indefinable objectives because, as theorists, and together with many other theorists, we must somehow sneak between Baudrillard the cultural theorist, the photographer, and his now posthumous selfhood, to advance his life's work and to observe how we have to move it forwards. Indeed, even the signs in the street and elsewhere that we were tracking appeared to perceive through the heat and throughout the afternoon that the objectives of our actions were not just conceived of by our freedom to follow the signs to Baudrillard's grave or by our capricious thoughts. We had a hunch that the Parisian landscape around us, that something about our entrance into the space of the Cimetière Montparnasse, offered a number of possible alternative objectives and trajectories, which we might or might not pursue.

Hence, and much like Baudrillard's (1993: 156–60) "Pursuit in Venice," wherein he describes artist Sophie Calle's *La Suite vénitienne*, her trailing and photographing in Venice of a man she hardly knew, we chose on this burning August day in Paris to provide some additional elements to both their literary and artistic endeavors. Certainly, it seemed as though we were not only doubling Baudrillard's commentary on Calle's work but also doubling Calle's own following and photographing of a man she did not really know. But we did so by tracking and photographing in Paris the signs to Baudrillard's grave, to a man we knew only though more signs, in the shape of his many influential books, articles, and photographs. Pursuit in Paris.

In time, we found the Boulevard Edgar-Quinet and the Entrée Principale to Cimetière Montparnasse, where Baudrillard was buried on March 13, 2007.

Histoire de Paris
Cimetière du Montparnasse

des terrains appartenant à l'Hôtel-Dieu et aux gieux de l'hôpital de la Charité, s'élevait depuis XVe siècle un moulin, transformé en guinguette rès la Révolution, à l'époque où abondaient barets, bals et restaurants près des barrières Montparnasse et du Maine. Lorsque la Ville e Paris décida, le 24 juillet 1824, d'ouvrir sur es vastes terrains le nouveau cimetière du Montparnasse, ce moulin devint la maison du gardien ; réduit à l'état de tour, il en reste un

Venturing beyond the huge gates, past several other scattered
tourists and an assortment of individuals and groups clearly visiting
their loved ones, and into the office of the Poste de Garde beside
the Entrée Principale, we asked about Baudrillard's location in
Cimetière Montparnasse. We were summarily directed to another
sign, to the large visual Plan du Cimetière standing at the head of
the Avenue Principale.

We wanted nothing except to discover the whereabouts of
Baudrillard's tomb. We had no other wish than to know where he
was buried. As Baudrillard was not listed on the Plan du Cimetière
Montparnasse, and as the Poste du Garde was less than forthcoming
about his location, we thought we might try to find Baudrillard's
grave unaided. This, however, soon proved to be something of a
disaster in a cimetière of such enormity, even if we did recognize,
in passing, through the small crowd gathered around it, the joint
burial place (20th division, grave 1) of the French existential philosopher Jean-Paul Sartre and the feminist writer Simone de Beauvoir.
"CAN YOU TELL ME WHERE CAMUS IS BURIED? I'M
HERE TILL SATURDAY 4TH. CHEERS. BENJAMIN," said
another sign, in capitals, a note held down by a stone on Sartre
and de Beauvoir's grave, continuing with the final and obviously
learned flourish: "P.S. Well done on *Being and Nothingness*."

But Sartre and de Beauvoir's tombs held little appeal for us on this particular journey, and so we strolled over to the office of the Conservation on the Avenue du Boulevart, where the names and the locations of the dead in Cimetière Montparnasse are kept.

"The name of the deceased?" said the middle-aged woman in glasses behind the front desk. "Jean Baudrillard," we said, in unison. She then spent a moment or two overcoming several psychological dilemmas involving, first, comprehending such a strange request from two, by now, bewildered and very clearly British tourists fluent only in Franglais, and, second, understanding why we were looking for the grave of someone who was obviously of no importance to either France or Britain. To stop us from disrupting her work any further and to keep us on the path of Baudrillard, she swiftly turned, dipped her bespectacled head and hands into the top drawer of a dark-green filing cabinet, and returned with the details on a yellow card. "Voila," she said. Having queried a number of signs and a range of individuals in and around Cimetière Montparnasse, we were now, at last, in a position to visit Baudrillard's tomb. We knew he was buried in the 8th division. We even knew the precise "ligne" of Baudrillard's grave (3 Sud), and set off to discover the position of his "concession" (7 Est) in order that we could pay our last respects to him and to his work and perhaps to take a few photographs of the tomb.

Turning left as we exited the Conservation and left again onto the Avenue Principale, we headed south in the high temperature, past more tourists and local visitors, past the sign for the Avenue du Nord and that of the Allée Lenoir to the point where the statue of the Genie du Sommeil éternel meets the Avenue Transversale. Turning right, we sought out the sign for the Allée des sergents de la Rochelle, 8th division. And, all of a sudden, there it was.

Now, surely, it was simply a matter of finding the correct line and the correct number of Baudrillard's grave. But what did *we* want from these lines and numbers, from these signs? What were we expecting Baudrillard's tomb to do for *us*? Did we want our arrival at his grave to justify our pursuit? Was our quest in fact in poor taste? Clearly, we wanted something out of it, even if it was only to satisfy our longing for the dark romance of Cimetière Montparnasse. And, of course, we imagined that Baudrillard, if he were there with us, might have criticized our physical and metaphysical search when, as regular tourists, there were so many other Parisian scenes to explore and so many other objectives and possibilities to delve into even within Montparnasse itself. Were we in suspense that our actions would unexpectedly become imperative, become, as Lingis has it, swayed by our perception of what was instantaneous, significant, and essential? Resembling many other pursuits, then, ours too had its underlying imperatives. Baudrillard's always already imminent cultural theory, we said, remains important. And not just important to us, here, right now, in Cimetière Montparnasse. We have, we said, to develop it because, in conjunction with innumerable others in cultural and visual theory, in philosophical, literary, sociological, political, and geographical studies, we are the ones who are here now and because we can. Everything that happens from this point on, we said, must therefore ease links and relations between Baudrillardian scholars. The mysteries of his cultural theory must not be kept but exposed. For the likely consequences of not acting as we felt we had to, of not acting at all, were, we worried, of a descent into or the return of the triteness of pre-Baudrillardian cultural and visual theory. Try to imagine, we said, echoing "Clarence," James Stewart's whimsical angel, (second class), in Frank Capra's (1946) film *It's a Wonderful Life*, the landscape of contemporary cultural and visual theory *as if Baudrillard had never existed*. Unthinkable, we agreed.

Evidently, there was nothing alive among the tombs of the 8th division for Baudrillard, for the individual whose sign we were tracking, and who had himself already reached the end of the line much earlier than many of us would have wished for. Yet Baudrillard's death has left a series of footprints that darken the entirety of the future of postmodern cultural and visual theory. We, as his sign's pursuers, were attempting, then, to follow in its footsteps. Stumbling around the graves of the 8th division, we finally managed to locate "ligne 3 Sud," "tombe 7 Est." Situated between Yvette Bares (1925–2007) on the left, facing the tombs from the front, and the perhaps stillborn infant Aymeric Bernier (2003–2003) on the right, Baudrillard's concrete grave, barely four months old, and thus on the day still without a formal headstone, abruptly came into view.

We had imagined that we would initially say a few words of remembrance and reflect on Baudrillard's contribution to contemporary cultural and visual theory. But it has to be admitted that, instead, visuality consumed us and we began photographing Baudrillard's tomb relentlessly.

Of course, we were not acting as we felt we had to earlier. In truth, we were not acting at all in the manner we had expected to. Yet, in taking these photographs, we did not feel that our actions were voyeuristic. Nor were our actions aimed at contributing to the, by now, substantial archive of photographs of Baudrillard. Undoubtedly, it was not the layout of the grave, with its large plant and terracotta plant pot, its wilting, almost indefinable, red and purple flowers, its smaller red and even smaller black plastic plant pots, and its modest, marble, silver, and black embossed signage, joined by a lonely seashell, "Jean BAUDRILLARD 1929 2007," that determined what we did that afternoon. Our imperative was not determined by the physical layout of Baudrillard's tomb. Its seemingly uncomplicated communication was that, at this graveside, at three o'clock on August 1, 2007, in the blazing Parisian sunlight, our attendance and actions involved envisaging the current layout of Baudrillard's tomb in relation to the future of cultural theory and of visual culture. But, simultaneously, and in this ostensibly clear-cut case, our imperative also communicated the fact that the purpose of being there, in Cimetière Montparnasse, on that particular afternoon, was not to "see" Baudrillard, since he was not "really" there. Instead, our imperative told us that we were the ones who had followed his sign because we viewed Baudrillard's cultural oeuvre, his theoretical object, as separable from the man himself. That is, we visualized it as being able to move others and us and of challenging or even superseding alternative cultural oeuvres and theoretical objects.

What was of importance, therefore, was not that we were tracking Baudrillard's dual existence, namely, of Baudrillard the "real" man and Baudrillard the "virtual" cultural theorist as it were. Rather, it was that our pursuit of both Baudrillard and his sign provided what was in fact the doubling of sensation. It was the sense that our relationship to him and to his sign was at once of the present and of the future. At this point, it occurred to us, the thought processes, sentences, and actions of the most common people, of British tourists in Paris even, might be portrayed not so much as ordinary but as gateways to the future. For these deliberations, sentences, and actions anticipate their final meaning from the very last words of such people, from the ultimate words that they will eventually utter and the final phrase that they will exclaim. In other words, we had surrendered to that bizarre curiosity which had initially provoked us to visit Baudrillard's grave.

We did not feel that Baudrillard existed for us at the graveside or that we had somehow become acquainted with him. More exactly, we felt that although Baudrillard no longer exists, we had at least managed to pursue his sign. Were our objectives, our utterances, as always to some extent, meaningless, fleeting, doomed, or were they simply lost in the storm of human (mis)understanding? Was this really the way to reveal some of the mysteries of Baudrillard's cultural and visual theory? Or should we have thought more of how all the signs we had just encountered in and around Cimetière Montparnasse seemed to recognize each other, seemed to be endlessly proclaiming their individual and shared identities? Much like the structuralist cultural theory of the sign, then, first identified by Ferdinand de Saussure (1966 [1915]), the creator of structural linguistics, the signs we had just stumbled upon were now the chief components of our language and communication. Each sign was thus not merely composed of a signifier, of an auditory image, or sound, and a signified or mental idea. It was also composed of a physical and psychological association between the parts of the sign and between each sign itself that was eternally random or conventional only within the terms of the language and communication we adopted on the day of our visit to Cimetière Montparnasse. Could we be certain that we had encountered Baudrillard at the graveside or had established for ourselves that he had ever existed? For nothing could be more uncertain, in French or English, than the black words "Jean BAUDRILLARD" and the black numbers "1929" and "2007," embossed on a silver plaque, and mounted on white marble.

Indeed, such words and numbers are composed of mere sounds, of the mere concept of a particular person, of a specific cultural and visual theorist, and of a particular period, of, in short, a subject, and an object, which we had long respected.

Then again, we reasoned, if the object of our pursuit was in part to disclose a few of the mysteries of Baudrillard's cultural and visual theory, did it matter whether or not he had ever existed? Perhaps because we did not really know him, only his oh-so French concepts, and perhaps because we did not really want to know him, only his sign, we were free of Baudrillard the man. We were, then, from this point on, should we choose to be, free to recognize only the sound or signifier associated with the *différance* (Derrida, 1976 [1967]), with the difference, with the now eternally deferred meaning of the sign "Jean BAUDRILLARD 1929 2007." Baudrillard signified, understood as referring to the object, to the material reality of his own corporeality, at this instant, therefore, barely existed. Yet, now that we had attempted to move toward the sign "Jean BAUDRILLARD 1929 2007," the question, which remained in the air, was whether we knew him any better than we had done before our visit to his tomb or better than anyone else who had not visited it? Maybe, we said, we should desert Baudrillard's graveside and, in the process, put an end to our own pursuit in Paris? For, in keeping with the imperatives in things, we had consequently been acting, responding to, and carving our way through a city space, acting and reacting to an imperative that, possibly always, everywhere, subordinates our present concerns to those of the future. Inexorably, then, and in struggling to enter into Baudrillard's trajectory, we two had not been using signs, words, and numbers to simply identify the things nearby or to make them or him visible. To be more precise, we had been invoking Baudrillard's absence and utilizing a kind of sign language as our main means of putting in place the objectives of our actions.

As a result, the only method by which we could actually meet "Jean BAUDRILLARD 1929 2007" was to pursue this sign consistent with a rule in opposition to the rule of the signified, where we would have followed Baudrillard so that we did not lose sight of the object Baudrillard, of the material reality of the man himself. Yet, inherent in our situation was the extraordinary instant when

"Jean BAUDRILLARD 1929 2007," as the referential aspect of the sign being pursued, was abruptly, if abstractly, signified. In fact, the sign "Jean BAUDRILLARD 1929 2007" was, rapidly, structurally, and linguistically, exposed not as the goal of our exploration or even as the explanation of the systematic relations of the structure of our particular sign language that afternoon, but, instead, as a mere tool that we had used to arrange the pace of our actions. Aware that we had not been following Baudrillard but the sign of Baudrillard, we were also aware that, as his sign's pursuers, to be sure, such a tool, such words and numbers, could also misrepresent our intentions and maneuvers. What if the imperatives in things were inverted? What if this tool, these words, and numbers that were apparently ordering our actions were in fact the orders and actions of the object, of the silver plaque, mounted on white marble? What if we were using this tool, these words, these numbers, less for presenting proposals about the world of cultural and visual theory to one another than for performing actions bordering on a haunting in which we endeavored to cajole the now eerie sign "Jean BAUDRILLARD 1929 2007" to flee from the house of postmodern cultural and visual theory? The really strange moment in our pursuit in Paris, therefore, was its unforeseen misrepresentation of Baudrillard, whose sign apparently persisted upon discerning our real objectives and operations whatever the cost.

In our pursuit in Paris, then, the imperatives in things were not only open to misrepresentation but also to inversion. Furthermore, such imperatives seemed to confirm de Saussure's central analytical insight that, as in the case of the sign "Jean BAUDRILLARD 1929 2007," everything in its language and numbers only functioned as it did because of its relation to some other words and numbers, which they were not, such as "Paul VIRILIO 1932 —," perhaps, or for which they can be substituted.

Consequently, and despite our inveigling at, protests against, enticements, and even intimidation of the sign "Jean BAUDRILLARD 1929 2007," of its language and numbers, of its hazy *différance*, its radical negativity continued to question us. It asked us whether, as theorists, we really wanted to go on seeing contemporary culture and visuality as nothing but a compound of material human activities, inexplicable artistic customs, and erotic tales, conventional landscapes, civilizing traditions, and routine constellations of images. Such a question was uncomfortable for us, since a positive answer entailed the potential abolition of a different conception of culture and visuality, of culture and visuality, as Clifford Geertz (1973: 89) has suggested, as systems of "inherited conceptions expressed in symbolic forms by means of which people communicate, perpetuate, and develop their knowledge about and attitudes toward life." Certainly, it involved the possible elimination of Geertz's (1973: 44) idea of culture and visuality as a set of control devices, as procedures, formulas, systems, orders, and codes for the management of human behavior.

Yet, as we both knew, the radically negative sign "Jean BAUDRILLARD 1929 2007," always, and everywhere, embodies within it the danger of the symbolic murder of all conventional notions of cultural and visual meaning (Baudrillard and Zurbrugg, 1993: 171). Accordingly, our nervousness about this sign rotated completely around its fierce relationship to culture, its distancing from visuality, its distrust, and, in fact, its rejection of culture *tout court*, of a "radicalness," of a claim, and of a pataphysical training, that not only does not want culture but also wants to "spit on it" (Baudrillard and Lotringer, 1993: 105). Such nervousness had little to do with the fact that, as cultural and visual theorists, as part of the culture industry, as British university lecturers, there was the very real possibility of being exposed by the sometimes-terrifying sign that is "Jean BAUDRILLARD 1929 2007." More readily, our nervousness had much to do with the fact that, as cultural and visual theorists, and, yes, as part of the culture industry, as university lecturers, both Baudrillard's and our own language directs the actions of others. For what we, as opposed to the sign "Jean BAUDRILLARD 1929 2007," were and are seeking to prevent in our everyday lives is the disparagement of cultural tasks that are, for us at least, vital and pressing. The construction of affirmative visual symbols, we said, is important, as is the transmission of a self-confident culture to young people in conjunction with our and their consumption of productive cultural meanings. Cultured individuals and theoretical institutions that order, such as universities, we said, are imperative, despite our growing distrust of their immediate economic priorities, and our increasing rejection of their seemingly unrelenting yet nearly always utilitarian political demands on knowledge creation. We could not go on pursuing the sign "Jean BAUDRILLARD 1929 2007." It was making us edgy. It was making us doubt whether we really wanted to be there, hovering around it. It was making us dwell on ourselves at that moment as humans who live in communities, visual cultures, political and economic environments which, to us, had and have important and immediate objectives.

We had then encountered the sign "Jean BAUDRILLARD 1929 2007," we had perceived it, and we had even conversed with it. But, in our circumstances at any rate, what the encounter with it had produced in us was a previously unconscious form of uneasiness. The sign "Jean BAUDRILLARD 1929 2007" was not the one whose fate we wanted to become. As part of our pursuit in Paris, we had, therefore, reacquainted ourselves with the *différance*, with the sheer indeterminacy that is the sign "Jean BAUDRILLARD 1929 2007" and even attempted a kind of conversation with it, by entering into its urban and cultural space, by attempting to enter into and perhaps divulge a handful of its mysteries. But, as passionate members of an ever more endangered and browbeaten academic community, we knew that we would remain forever separate from it. For we did not want to participate in a dialog with it as fellow denigrators of culture and visuality. If possible, we wanted to enter a dialog with such signs as fervent members of an academic community of resistance, of one that is aimed at preserving its history, which wants to renew, even double, its commitment to the exploration of postmodern culture and the language of visual imagery. In the end, then, we could not fully support the sign "Jean BAUDRILLARD 1929 2007." Yet nor did we wish to annihilate the trail of this important intellectual shooting star, or exterminate its specific sound. For these reasons, we sought, if not to change the many and ultimately undecidable meanings of the sign "Jean BAUDRILLARD 1929 2007," then to continually question it, to hear different sounds, and to communicate different, and, yes, deferred meanings. As a result, and although the sign "Jean BAUDRILLARD 1929 2007" was the one which we had been pursuing all afternoon, we were now asking it to follow us in our own quest to re-empower, culturally, politically, economically, a vulnerable and demoralized academic community that is critical and immediately under threat in Britain and elsewhere in terms of its traditional objectives.

But the sign "Jean BAUDRILLARD 1929 2007" must have rejected or misunderstood our request, since it remained the linguistic and numerical sign that we had first come across. It could not be depicted or represented in any other way except as "Jean BAUDRILLARD 1929 2007." Its imperatives, its measure of culture, its formulation of visual language, we said, ultimately, would always be foreign to our own. Our camera shutter release button fingers, our arms, our legs, and our feet, were tired from our afternoon's walk in the hot Parisian sun. Yet, even at that point, we still had no desire to obliterate the sign "Jean BAUDRILLARD 1929 2007," only to posit other ways of organizing human cultural actions, to imagine other and, perhaps, more encouraging ways of attaining the objectives of cultural and visual theory.

We had not set out on our pursuit in Paris with the intention of ensnaring the sign "Jean BAUDRILLARD 1929 2007." On balance, we had always assumed that we had an empathy with this particular sign, an empathy that, whilst never unconditional, all the same, would continue until the end of the line. But we found that we could no longer easily or fully accept it. Yet our imperative did not seek to exert its power over it or to extinguish its words and numbers. For ours was a contradictory response. On the one hand, we wanted to make the sign "Jean BAUDRILLARD 1929 2007" advance into infinity, to open up new fields of cultural and visual theory for new and never-ending cultural actions and creative actors. But, on the other, we also wanted to make its words, its numerical inscriptions, stop, right there and then, so that, as Baudrillard (1987) himself advised in his *Forget Foucault*, we could stop thinking about it and about him. This contradictory response regarding the sign "Jean BAUDRILLARD 1929 2007," of seeking both its infinite progression and its imminent inertia, was not a requirement for us. It was not a calculation on our part. Rather, we wanted to unite these two words, these two numbers, not with the death of an infamous cultural theorist and visionary but with other, perhaps alternative words and numbers, with other cultural perspectives and visual systems. However, this was something that, we were quite sure, would not have pleased the sign "Jean BAUDRILLARD 1929 2007" whether in its progressive or its inert phase. Even so, our imperative had no obvious yearning to see the downfall of this sign. Instead, it had a desire, as William Merrin (2005) has written elsewhere, to stop its seemingly permanent yet also self-imposed isolation from mainstream media and cultural studies and from a considerable number of other individual cultural and visual signs, theories, and academic disciplines in the present period. In consequence, it was not a question of trying to predict, for instance, which cultural or visual sign would appear at the top of the contemporary hierarchy of cultural signs the longest this academic season. Nor was it a question of which theoretical caste would inhabit the space of, say, visual culture the most securely, or even of which disciplinary class would be permitted to speak to young people and to others the most loudly. Alternatively, it was a question of asking which signs were and are being erased? Which theoretical castes are open to the cultural space, to the visual world of the sign "Jean BAUDRILLARD 1929 2007," and which disciplinary classes seek to deprive it, to silence it, at the very time when it has turned into one of the few remaining signs of radical *différance*?

Certainly, we had not come to Cimetière Montparnasse merely to describe the linguistic functioning of or to expunge the sign "Jean BAUDRILLARD 1929 2007." We were neither its protectors nor its enemies. We were not interested in irritating it or in persuading it to wish for, or to assent to, its own symbolic ruin. For our imperative wanted to open up a cultural space, a phenomenology of perception, where the sign "Jean BAUDRILLARD 1929 2007" would reveal the order of the post-theoretical, or even the order intrinsic to the contemporary cultural and visual world and which we perceive of as hyperdisciplinary. We were, then, we decided, members of a disciplinary class that wants to reveal both the order and the thought processes that are governed by the imperatives in things. That is to say, we are members of a disciplinary class that, bodily, and, yes, sensually and emotionally, is an opponent of all those who seek not to converse with others but to stifle them. In other words, we said, our pursuit in Paris had been frequently regulated by the imperatives in things, by the things that had come from the world of the boulevards of Montparnasse and the Cimetière all around us.

Throughout our phenomenological odyssey, then, we had drawn on our own life experiences, on the directives in the natural and the urban world, and on our exchanges with others. Such exchanges shaped not only our thought and behavior on that day but also our language. Yet prior to our language, which existed as a mere exchange of signs, or our faces as further exterior signs, there was also the glow in our eyes. Moreover, beneath our apparently lucid and discursive community of two was another community of the dead that insisted that we bare ourselves to Baudrillard, to the one, as Lingis (1994) might put it, with which we had nothing in common, to Baudrillard the outsider. Accordingly, we encountered the sign "Jean BAUDRILLARD 1929 2007" physically, as part of our inner muscular schema of motion, affectively, as a rush and uproar in the sphere of the emotions, ethically, as the imperative to moral admiration and our own educational responsibility, and, finally, as an impediment to our vacation-induced decadence. Our language on that day was thus not essentially a means of recognition but a means of struggle with and the sanctification of the words and work of mourning. Our language emerged out of this affective materiality, this elemental sonority of the earth, out of the urban birdsong, out of tourists' chatter, and out of our own whispers. Neither laughing nor crying, consecrating or desecrating, our imperative conveyed not a meaning but an ambiance, a power, and a pulsation. And it was through these disturbances, commotions Lingis (1994: 69–106) calls "the murmur of the world," that the sign "Jean BAUDRILLARD 1929 2007," the other as such, and our own singularities, could be felt, and that we could be there for him, for us, and for others, and to stand beside him, even as our words faltered.

Yet both the most important advantage and disadvantage of the sign "Jean BAUDRILLARD 1929 2007," we said, remains. And they are that whilst it invokes an estimable strangeness from other signs, it is also ultimately incomprehensible and to a significant degree unusable as a sign because it continues to challenge any attempt at or sense of unity with any other cultural signs, with any other perspectives on visual culture. Such is the enigma of the figure of its radical *différance*, we determined, of the fact that it can neither and on no account only or merely be imagined as the opposite of other signs nor be imagined as identical to other signs. For to conceive of the sign "Jean BAUDRILLARD 1929 2007" opposed to another sign, such as "Paul VIRILIO 1932 —," for example, would be to lock it in a particular position regarding, say, visual culture, and thus limit what, we at length agreed, actually characterizes it, which is a remarkable suspension, a growing mobilization, and a continually deferred apartness. As its very processes appeared to have been demonstrating all afternoon, then, the sign "Jean BAUDRILLARD 1929 2007" is, in the end, an alternative term both for unity with other cultural perspectives and visual systems and for a radical yet negative difference from them.

By means only of a silent glance into the luminosity in each other's eyes and a left-inclined toss of one of our heads, we finally decided to leave Baudrillard's grave. Tiptoeing as respectfully as we could between the tombs of line 3 Sud in the 8th division and back onto the Allée des Sergents de la Rochelle, returning along the Avenue Transversale, and the Avenue Principale, we left Cimetière Montparnasse through the Entrée Principale and arrived back onto Boulevard Edgar-Quinet. Catching sight of a street café, a few tables, and some chairs on the pavement about two hundred and fifty meters off to the right, we chose to rest up awhile and buy a cold drink. After all, it was four o'clock in the hot afternoon in Paris and we didn't feel like doing very much.

Note

1 I would like to thank Alphonso Lingis for our conversations and for inadvertently inspiring this chapter and Ryan Bishop, Mike Featherstone, Douglas Kellner, and Joanne Roberts for commenting on earlier drafts. All the photographs contained in this chapter are by and copyright of John Armitage and Joanne Roberts.

References

Baudrillard, J. (1987) *Forget Foucault*. New York: Semiotext(e).

Baudrillard, J. (1991) *Seduction*. Montreal: St Martin's Press.

Baudrillard, J. (1993) "Pursuit in Venice," in: *The Transparency of Evil: Essays on Extreme Phenomena* (J. Baudrillard). pp. 156–160. London: Verso.

Baudrillard, J. and Lotringer, S. (1993) "Forget Baudrillard," in: M. Gane (ed.) *Baudrillard Live: Selected Interviews*. pp. 99–127. London: Routledge.

Baudrillard, J. and Zurbrugg, N. (1993) "Fractal Theory," in: M. Gane (ed.) *Baudrillard Live: Selected Interviews*. pp. 165–171. London: Routledge.

Derrida, J. (1976 [1967]) *Of Grammatology*. Baltimore, MD: Johns Hopkins University Press.

Geertz, C. (1973) *The Interpretation of Cultures*. New York: Basic Books.

Levinas, E. (1969) *Totality and Infinity*. Pittsburgh, PA: Duquesne University Press.

Lingis, A. (1994) "The Murmur of the World," in: *The Community of Those Who Have Nothing in Common* (A. Lingis). pp. 69–106. Bloomington and Indianapolis, IN: Indiana University Press.

Lingis, A. (1998) *The Imperative*. Bloomington and Indianapolis, IN: Indiana University Press.

Merleau-Ponty, M. (1968) *The Visible and the Invisible*. Evanston, IL: Northwestern University Press.

Merrin, W. (2005) *Baudrillard and the Media: A Critical Introduction*. Cambridge: Polity.

Saussure, F. de (1966 [1915]) *A Course in General Linguistics*. London: Collins.

Film

Capra, F. (1946) *It's a Wonderful Life*. Liberty films/RKO Pictures.

7

What is a Tank?

Ryan Bishop and John Phillips

(© Craig DeBourbon)

Introduction

The *tank* might be thought to function as a prosthetic extension of both human sensation and action. In this respect, it may have

served the British psychoanalyst Wilfred Bion, while in the tank
corps during World War I, as a disturbing catalyst for his questions concerning knowledge formation and the development of
intellectual, critical thought. It also provides a vehicle for this
chapter's inquiry into Baudrillard's thoughts on simulation, death,
and hyperreality, which can be seen as echoing indirectly Bion's
engagement with sensate experience as a kind of prosthesis-at-the-
origin. The technical development of the tank since World War I
corresponds in precise ways with the intensification of both technological and experiential mutations in the fields concerned with
sensate production and manipulation (e.g. televisual and electro-
acoustic technologies). Yet it also evokes something archaic in the
experience of the world, which, at each stage, follows a pattern of
defense and projection, projection and defense, in a circular logic
that only in its failure to complete itself leaves open the possibility
for what we could call, in the strict historical sense, an *event*.

In the late work, *The Intelligence of Evil or the Lucidity Pact*,
Baudrillard argues that a "great game" has replaced the previously absolute distinction, made possible by the existence of God,
between divine and empirical reality. This distinction has been
eclipsed by a new one that distinguishes "the integral drive" from
"the dual drive." Baudrillard writes that:

> The very idea of completion, of Integral Reality, is unbearable, but the
> dual form, the form that denies any final reconciliation, any definitive
> accomplishment, is also very difficult – and perhaps even impossible –
> to conceive in its radicalism. And yet it is this lucid vision of an endless
> revision, in this denial of any objective solution, that the intelligence
> of evil, if it exists, is grounded. (22)

The mobilization of Integral Reality – that is, "a Virtual Reality
that rests on the deregulation of the very reality principle" (17)
– in its most virulent global forms results in the other portion of
the great game, the dual drive, which is a negative reaction to the
other's totalizing powers. The Integral Reality creates its own
outside, its own resistance, in the form of evil. But "to speak evil"
is only to point out the self-defeating nature of a fundamentalist,
all-encompassing view of reality, and paradoxically, to reinforce its

very operation. Therefore, to speak evil is not resistance at all but perpetuation of the Integral Reality in the mock struggle, or great game, between Integral Reality and a dual drive. Integral Reality spawns its own resistance, thereby absorbing into itself any attempt to resist it or to engage it critically.

It is not difficult to see that the apparently recent emergence of this new *agonism* simulates in its blank parody a former *antagonism* between what Baudrillard once described as the first two orders of simulacra: between those that "aim for the restitution or the ideal institution of nature made in God's image" and those that are "founded on energy, force, its materialization by the machine" (1994: 121). We will try to render the implications of this analysis a little clearer.

As is well known, Baudrillard opposes simulation to representation. He understands the opposition in terms of a kind of permanent struggle in which the one is hell bent on absorbing or otherwise negating the other and vice versa. Moreover he understands the struggle not in abstract or universal terms but as the mediation of historicity itself, and so it becomes manifest in historical conditions and historical struggles, not least in those that dominate today in the guise of the image, the chief vehicle of both representation *and* simulation.

The image, no less than the sign, has possibly always been the site of severe struggle. Baudrillard charts four of what he calls "successive phases of the image," which describe the changing fortunes of representation and simulation. If representation begins by dominating and simulation wins in the end, this is only to the extent that the successive stages describe not a progression but a circle in whose beginning and end one finds *nothing* or *death*, a sphere that is so devoid of significant differences that it is swallowed up in some unthinkable (whether absolutely profound or totally superficial) Real. The circle begins with the theological notion of a non-sensuous *signified* suspicious of all *signifiers* that might, even with the utmost respect and diffidence, do service in its representation, and ends with a signifier that serves only the generation of further signifiers with no reference to and certainly no respect for anything beyond the signifying system that it would have otherwise served as its representation.

The struggle between representation and simulation takes several shapes, of course, but Baudrillard identifies amongst his initial examples the religious distrust of images: "the stakes," he says, "will always have been the murderous power of images, murderers of the real, murderers of their own model, as the Byzantine icons could be those of divine identity" (1994: 5). Nevertheless, as Western history particularly informs us, several kinds of negating and mediating dialectic are available to rescue the Real and its notions from the threat inherent in the necessity of representation. "Western faith and good faith," he argues, "became engaged in this wager on representation: that a sign could be exchanged for meaning and that something could guarantee this exchange – God, of course" (1994: 5). It is important, then, to grasp that simulation as such is not a new phenomenon, just arrived on the scorched earth in the wake of virtual reality, the digital image and *The Matrix*. Representation depends on the possibility of simulation yet must always keep it under control, in the domestic service of various conceptions of truth and interpretation.

An historical analysis would show, however, that the declining fortunes of representation and its values really begin to take effect during the nineteenth century in two powerful yet mutually antagonistic forms (as will always have been the pattern) of critical production: those of science – in fierce repudiation of metaphysical notions, whether ideal or romantic, that still cling to the nineteenth-century imagination – and those of iconoclastic or eschatological styled philosophy – in the guise of Nietzsche's will to power, for instance, or Freud's unconscious, conceptions that dislodge the very concept itself to replace it with forces and plays of force. Nietzsche and Freud, of course, do not inaugurate the age of simulacra and the Hyperreal, with their alternately joyful or mournful affirmations of substitution and the loss of the real, any more than do the efforts of an increasingly dominant empirical or formalist scientific outlook whose dream is a complete theoretical, encyclopedic knowledge. Nevertheless the process has begun, and the image no longer serves as the representation of a profound and/or divine real. It now serves in the struggle between a science of the real and its critical discontents. It is this struggle, rather precisely, that is performed, according to Baudrillard, as the great game.

The phases of the image can be refined in terms of what Baudrillard calls the "three orders of simulacra," if we accept that the first order is itself "founded on the image" (1994: 121). The Nietzschean overturning of the image thus shares with its supposed antagonist in science an inevitable drive towards "continuous expansion" (121) but this is still only as the "second order" of simulacra. Baudrillard's account of the great game is an account of what happens when the antagonism, the mutual incompatibility, of the two orders (the order that serves truth and the order that serves production and expansion) is simulated, when the two sides are no more than actors in a simulation of the struggle itself.

If this eclipse of the first order of simulacra, Baudrillard argues in his 2005 book, leaves us "up against reality," then the eclipse of the second leaves us up against an apparently barely speakable danger. To speak the danger is to participate in the great game itself, an intensified third order of simulacra, "the simulacra of simulation," or the "cybernetic game" (1994: 121). What is at stake in the earlier work is the gap or distance that is always threatened with abolition or reabsorption in the passage between orders (so that the simulacra of the first naturalist order tend to be reabsorbed in the Promethean second). This gap or distance between orders always under threat of reabsorption "on behalf of the model" (or cybernetic hyperreality) is what leaves room for "an ideal or critical projection" (1994: 122). The possibility of such a projection – the space or distance between orders – has in fact itself been reabsorbed in the endless simulacra of the great game, where the totalization project includes its opposite or evil as a function of its own logic.

Baudrillard perhaps then evokes the apparition of an intellectual space that would, if it existed, engage the so-called great game without participating in it. The only mode of defense would thus be non-participation. *The Intelligence of Evil* may offer a defensive move of this kind, against the great game, by attempting to think and operate outside of it, or at least to think that possibility without even putting it into words as such. In Baudrillard's terms, then, this possibility must remain in doubt, a closely guarded secret or rumor that must nonetheless somehow "get out." This mode of defense would need to reserve the space or the gap of critical projection without operating it – without using it up – thus keeping it back from its otherwise inevitable re-absorption. The defensive move thus attempts to hold back the realization of Integral Reality, to reserve without utilizing a critical power resistant to the drive for completion and its negative evil.

Tank

The tank by 1918 had improved over bulky and barely mobile arms carriers with limited fields of vision. It had a powerful purpose-built engine, as well as its own steering mechanism. It was increasingly reliable, mobile, and easy to control, although crews had to be adapted with special training for developing technological requirements. The latest tank (in the first decade of the twenty-first century) might be equipped with a CITV (commander's independent thermal viewer), which provides the commander with independent stabilized day and night vision, a 360-degree view, automatic sector scanning, automatic target cueing of the gunner's sight, and back-up fire control. The viewing capacities of the typical tank can be as much as ten times narrow field of view and three times wide field of view. And the thermal image would be displayed in the eyepiece of the gunner's sight. Yet, the tank's earliest avatar is a clumsily constructed iron vehicle mounted with various sizes of cannon that whole teams would find almost impossible to maneuver. In spite of its design and purpose, the earliest tank becomes a target and death-trap, its triumph greater in image and for propaganda than in effect. In several ways its presence announces not the current state but the future of technological warfare.

The first tank provided the immediate solution to a fundamental problem of trench warfare – getting the troops out of the trenches without having them mown down straight away – but did so only by making the trench mobile. The tank largely replicated the problem of trench warfare by taking the trench above ground, making it kinetic, and in the process transforming it into a mobile target for enemy fire. The earliest tank blindly trundled across "no man's land" only to be moored on the enemy's trenches (if it made it that far without being blown up or set aflame). The defensive move provided by the tank led to a whole set of new problems in need of refinement. The history of the tank provides a constant shifting between its manifestations as cobbled-together behemoth and as efficient battle machine, for once the offensive function is achieved, it immediately generates scores of new technological weaponry to neutralize its power. As such, the tank embodies unwittingly the inevitable failure in the drive toward completeness of battlefield technological supremacy.

The projection of the soldier and the military onto the battlefield in the form of mobile armor and mobilized firepower inevitably draws more and improved enemy firepower, rendering its offensive capacities irrelevant, forcing it to become a defensive machine again. The drive of military technology for the past two hundred years has been an ever-increasing visual control of the battlefield for the combatant and erasing it for the enemy and, in this manner, replicates the drives of integral reality. The tank carries these drives into the battlefield, prosthetically outfitted to see up to ten times more than the naked eye can observe. But the unfolding of the battlefield is always and evidently manipulated from a distance with the tank and those within it linked to an extraordinary set of IT and satellite links. The tank team works away surveying and controlling the terrain yet is controlled by the battery of tele-technologies and prosthetic extensions that allow for sensate action at a distance. The tank team carries into the battlefield a robust set of tele-technological systems designed to fulfill the dream of complete terrain control, the integral reality of combat scenes, and, in so doing, materializes the circular logic of projection and defense through the senses.

An example of the combined drive for ever-increasing visual control of the battlefield environment, as well as the circular logic of projection and defense operative in tank design, can be found in the following description of the MIA2 Abrams tank improved sighting system. The second generation of the forward looking infrared (FIIR) sighting system, according to the manufacturer and industry analysts, indicates a significant improvement over the first generation, in an attempt to secure complete visual domination of the terrain and represents one of the most significant upgrades in the Abrams top class tank, the MIA2.

The 2nd Gen FLIR is a fully integrated engagement-sighting system designed to provide the gunner and tank commander with significantly improved day and night target acquisition and engagement capability. This system allows 70% better acquisition, 45% quicker firing and greater accuracy. In addition, a gain of 30% greater range for target acquisition and identification will increase lethality and lessen fratricide. The Commander's Independent Thermal Viewer (CITV) provides a hunter killer capability. The 2nd Gen FLIR is a variable power sighting system ranging from 3 or 6 power (wide field of view) for target acquisition and 13, 25 or 50 power (narrow field of view) for engaging targets at appropriate range.[1]

In its capacity as a multi-eyed fighting machine, the tank can alter the power of its lenses according to terrain and condition needs while at the same time making the terrain irrelevant by virtue of its being folded into the virtuality of the sighting system. Varied powers of both wide and narrow field viewing enhance the machine's capacity to kill the enemy while saving one's comrades a similar but far more ignominious fate: increased lethality and lessened fratricide. The battlefield's being more completely brought under tele-technological control, however, only signals the impossibility of the capacity to completely control it. The second generation signals that there will invariably be a third generation and many other subsequent ones. The announcement of previous and present failure resides in the announcement of the new generation as significant improvement.

Bion

Wilfred Bion began his career as a psychoanalyst having worked as a therapist with groups of traumatized ex-soldiers after World War I. Bion was fascinated by the psychological basis in sensations from early in his career (learning as much from neuroscience as from the philosophy he studied as a graduate at Oxford). In his clinical work, Bion established what we might now recognize as the essentially prosthetic nature of human sensation, on which is based experience and knowledge formation. The several sensation-distinctions that organize Bion's treatment of psychic experience operate in ways that foreshadow Baudrillard's discussions of the merging of biophysioanatomical sciences. Bion's theoretical discussions help to complicate distinctions between classical functionalism (the notion of the machine as an extension of the natural body or psyche) and what Baudrillard calls mortal "deconstruction": the "extension of death" that the body undergoes when its parts merge with, or are confused with, machine parts (as in his reading of J. G. Ballard's *Crash* from *Simulation and Simulacra*). Bion does not talk of lost unity (which Baudrillard believes still remains the horizon of psychoanalysis) but rather he talks, like Baudrillard himself, of psychic experience built out of disparate sensations through kinds of *projection* and *defense*. The notion of *projection* central to both thinkers (Bion's projective identification and Baudrillard's three orders of simulacra) serves as a kind of catastrophic mediation that "middles" rather than mediates.

For Bion the environment is characterized at the earliest stages by what he calls an "ambiance" that is structured by objects or things. This ambiance also represents the world of the psychotic patient. Bion talks of "the diffusion of sensuous particles" that, in the form of words, is projected into the inside of external objects, providing them with characteristics of whatever sense has been projected into them. If sight or hearing has been projected into an object, then this object will be experienced as looking at or listening to the person. These objects represent the furniture that normally outfits dreams, but with psychotic patients they function as part of their everyday life.

Even when not identified as psychotic, this environmental ambiance might function as a continuation of the dream state into the waking state. In a seminar from 1976 he talks about this in the context of sensation. The individual's three "long distance probes" – the senses of smell, eyesight, and hearing – are *very* sensitive, he says. These senses put the individual in touch with objects that are beyond physical contact and, perhaps, present things one doesn't want to see at all. "Suppose," he says, "it becomes really penetrating," and he provides an example:

There is a medieval drawing of a person shoving his head through a sort of adamantine shell and is then able to observe the universe that lies outside. If astronomy actually enabled the individual to penetrate into space, then there might easily be an objection to that – a violent objection against all these radio telescopes and so forth, a wish to destroy them all because they made life so uncomfortable – it is so much nicer to be blind and deaf. (Bion, 2005: 7)[2]

Un missionnaire du moyen âge raconte qu'il avait trouvé le point
où le ciel et la Terre se touchent...

From L'atmosphère: météorologie populaire, *by Camille Flammarion,*
1888. 163.

Bion's point here, confirmed when one makes reference to his clinical writings, would be that the inextricable attachment of psychic processes to sensations from the earliest stages of an individual's life means that a certain level of pain cannot be avoided.[3] "If you are not willing to pay the price of the inescapable fact of pain, then you get reduced to a situation in which you try to isolate yourself" (Bion, 2005: 5). Physical isolation might involve shutting yourself off from the world: "draw the blinds, turn out the lights, have the telephone cut off, stop reading the newspapers and keep yourself in a situation of complete isolation" (5). But mentally this is not possible by virtue of the long-distance probes, the senses, open uncontrollably at all times to pressures and sensations. The reference above (and throughout) to prosthetic tele-technologies is of course significant.[4] Bion speculates on the existence – acknowledged by embryologists – of the fetus's auditory and optic pits and the nasal passage, and he wonders when these actually become functional. "I think," he says, "that, at some point, the foetus can be so subjected to these changing pressures that long before it changes from a watery fluid to a gaseous one – the air, birth – it does its best to be rid of the whole lot" (6). For Bion, it is only by tolerating these pressures that a system of thinking can be developed. The impossible desire to be, as he puts it, blind and deaf, manifests not only in psychosis but also in dreams [but]:

> There are very few individuals who have any respect for the continu-
> ation of those dreams when they are wide awake. They are not even
> likely to admit having them, because they know that the rest of us will
> call them hallucinations or delusions – as we all know, the authorities
> in some places are at pains to shut people up where they can do little
> harm [. . .] inside mental institutions. (7–8)

His point is not so much to criticize the practice of incarceration but more to draw attention to several of the ways in which such "shutting in" or "shutting up" occurs, thus making thought – in certain situations – impossible. Drugs, including alcohol and other soporifics, would be one of the ways; but ideas themselves in certain conditions can have the same effect.

Bion's thoughts on prosthetic extension correspond to Baudrillard's identification of the body's "mortal deconstruction . . . not in the pejorative illusion of a lost unity of the subject (which is still the horizon of psychoanalysis), but in the explosive vision of a body delivered to 'symbolic wounds,' of a body confused with technology in its violating and violent dimension" (Baudrillard, 1994: 111). Baudrillard's own earlier speculations, especially in *The System of Objects*, are informed by the psychoanalytic accounts of paranoid projection, which allow the hypothesis that man projects his sexuality into his technologies in order to control it, to tame, it or to domesticate it. This is already a developed account of what (in *Symbolic Exchange and Death*) will become the second order of simulacra. Using Jacques Lacan's revision of Freud and concept of the *phallus* (the "signifier" as material image represented by the male sexual organ), Baudrillard's readings of robotic and automated technology especially illustrate this underlying hypothesis of projection. In *The System of Objects* he speculates that the narrative of the self-destructive robot in revolt represents the attempt by man to tame his own sexuality (the dangerous *phallus*); but that once projected onto the outside this is turned against him:

> If we carry the Freudian view to its logical conclusion, we cannot but wonder whether this is not man's way of using technology in its utmost demented incarnations to celebrate the future occurrence of his own death, his way of renouncing his own sexuality in order to be quit of all anxiety. (Baudrillard, 1996: 132)

So in the later reading of science fiction (from *Simulation and Simulacra*) a further development is necessary (corresponding with the third order). Tele-technologies, which already are prosthetic extensions of the body and the constituted self, have now developed so much of what the self invests in its objects that there is no functional difference between the two: no self, no object. The tank can thus be regarded as something like the symbolic extension of robotic, automated technology into the glorified, willed, death of the subject itself. Tanks are the projections, manifestations, or reflections of what Derrida calls "prosthetics at the origin," but they materialize a prosthetics destined to destroy itself. The projection of the senses into the battlefield outfits the tank as body; and a tank team is made up of the necessary parts of the functioning machine, the internal organs of the tank itself.

Just as the exoskeleton of the tank returns to its prosthetic origin to reveal the origin itself as prosthesis, so too the various tele-technologies return to their sensate origins. These projections, intended as defenses to protect the vulnerable self and body, also provide extensions to death – indeed they are also literally extensions of death. The supposed division between the rational body and the irrational one – in this "mortal destruction of the body" – disappears. The semiurgy of the body appears in the metallurgy of the tank.

Landscapes and Tanks

(© Chris Dobrowolski)

Chris Dobrowolski's *Landscape Escape 2* is a sculpture in the form of a tank constructed of Constable landscape reproductions and bits of garden machinery all purchased from car boot sales in and around Essex. The sculpture can actually move about, and fire shoots out of its mock gun barrel. Dobrowolski's sculpture conflates landscape, tank, and technologies of simulation, as well as the historicity of all these. If the tank is the trench made mobile, then Dobrowolski's sculptural tank is a pastoral made mobile, an extension of the landscape turned lethal, which is, of course, how a military tank affects its landscape: the battlefield. The very prostheses that allow the tank commander to lay bare the entire landscape for the tank's gunner, to render it as fully visible and therefore obscene, are those that attempt to contain and manufacture the entire battle process within integral reality.

"The prostheses of the industrial age," Baudrillard writes, in *Simulations and Simulacra*, "are still external, *exotechnical*. We are in the soft age of technologies – genetic and mental software. As long as these prostheses of the industrial golden age were mechanical, they still returned to the body to modify its image – conversely, they themselves were metabolized in the imaginary and this technological metabolism was also part of the image of the body" (Baudrillard,

1994: 100). The shift from the second order of simulation to the third is realized in our scenario in the image of the tank as body entering the landscape through the hardware and software that makes it all visible. We shift from Bion's energetic extension of the self in its tele-technologies to the unifying power of integral reality. The sensate experience itself is modified by the imaginary, the body recast as a mobile screen interacting with clearly articulated networks, the self a plasma afloat in a sea of endless extensions of which tank, prostheses, and landscape are but arbitrary boundaries. There is nothing but total immersion in hyperreality, in which "the routinized violence of war" has added to it "the equally routinized violence of the images" (Baudrillard, 2005: 77). Within integral reality, the brain itself has become a screen, and all of our senses are made aesthetic "in the worst sense of the term" (79).

Combining the Constable reproductions in the form of a tank, or as tank skin, Dobrowolski alludes obliquely to the iconography of tanks themselves while simultaneously commenting slyly on the conversion of nature into landscape as a site of war and a target for military technology. For the technology to perform as it should, the terrain must disappear, become irrelevant and immaterial via virtualization.

(© Eric van Straaten)

Thus, the many photos of tanks in advertisements by manufacturers, books by military historians, and websites by military enthusiasts show the tank in the landscape, running over it, whizzing through it, firing into it, emptying its armaments into its horizon with the frame often cropping any target, any enemy, any foe. The landscape itself seems targeted both materially (by the tank) and immaterially through its incorporation or absorption to different extents into the stages of simulation.

Dobrowolski's sculpture is, for one exhibition (in one of its poses), perched or wedged on a television. The tank becomes the bearer of realism into the battlefield, propped up by that most pervasive purveyor of hyperrealism and the immediacy of the hyperreal: the television. His tank, in this pose, seemingly combines all three levels of Baudrillard's simulation but in slightly problematic ways. The realism practiced by Constable apparently operates in the first order of the simulacra, in the classical tradition of mimesis, supposedly restoring through representation the ideal of nature as formed by God. But Constable's practice more directly aligns with the second order of the simulacra, the Nietzschean one found in "the materialization by the machine" of a productive order predicated on the unleashing of energy. Constable converting his rough sketches of landscapes into the vast realist canvases of nature exemplifies the Promethean unleashing of the forces of production to institute a regime of reproduction and simulation. By having his tank moored on a television, like a World War I tank wedged in the enemy trench, Dobrolowski emphasizes the tendency of the order of simulacra to absorb the gap found between one order and the next. The gap between them closes in the pincers of the integral reality's relentless drive to completion. The power of the third order, which is neither classical nor Nietzschean, is its capacity of absorption.

If Constable's apparent attempt to replicate created nature in realist painting actually manifests the steady release of productive energy, then he already displays the ease with which the first order and second order close, eliminating the gap between them. Dobrowolski's sculpture marks the productivity of the gap by detailing its closure. The gap between the first and second orders has been covered up by the reproduction as tank covering, land scape as camouflage, and mobility as wrecked on a delivery system of the electronic image. If camouflage is supposed to make the tank blend into its landscape, the realist paintings covering this tank make it stand out. That which is supposed to make nature invisible, as in the first order of simulation, in fact allows us to see the machine. By wearing its landscape on its skin, this tank enters its environment as the machinery of the simulacrum itself, as well as anything that is mobilized as defense against its order. The tank manifests the closed loop of projection and defense endlessly folding back onto itself, imagining an external reality (nature) wholly consumed by internal projections (simulation). In the complex interaction between reproductions and the tank, *Landscape Escape 2* performs as if the gap between orders of simulation remained open, as if in their confusion the always potentially traitorous power of representation and the productive force of the machine remained marked by a fundamental difference, which in the third order is threatened or already absorbed. *Landscape Escape 2* dramatizes this gap between orders of simulation, a gap where there may be a space for critical thought but which is endlessly appropriated by integral reality.

Conclusion

The great game takes the form of a quandary: the means to extract oneself from the integral reality driving the great game can only be found in that which cannot be used. The analogy between Baudrillard's account of the great game and the fortunes of the tank indicates a certain inevitability of failure that is nonetheless increasingly difficult to express. If the history and development of the tank are the inevitable result of attempts repeatedly to solve the problems of the scenarios of military engagement, then it not only exhibits the key principles according to which the technological sphere develops but it also indicates the ways available to anyone who wishes to engage this great game – the twin action of Integral Reality and Dual Drive. One would have to act in such a way that this inevitability is reserved, withdrawn even, from the game itself or held back from it, for it remains the last space of a critical response. However, no form of action that utilizes this space, if Baudrillard is correct, can be made that would not be immediately reappropriated to the game itself. Perhaps the maintenance of a gap or a failure, without putting it into action, remains the only task left for critical thought.

Somehow wedged between the first and second orders of simulacra, between the sorcery of forged images, false likenesses, and motorized, mass-produced machines, we are as if projected into the tank wedged across a TV. We can neither move forward to control our future, nor reach back as if to return to some idealized state. Such states are anyway endlessly simulated in the hyperreal. The imperative is twofold. First the simulations of the hyperreal must be exposed as such. But, second, our desires to denounce motorized and militarized technologies might be directed by the first side of this imperative, which would involve the acknowledgment that, in our very act of denunciation, the moral law rises up again (a law that in its politicized forms would regulate or control and thus manifest the forces it disapproves of) to confirm all the more powerfully the hyperreal itself.

Notes

1 http://www.globalsecurity.org/military/systems/ground/m1a2.htm.

2 Bion appears to be talking about the so-called "flammarion Woodcut," an anonymous wood engraving supposedly representing the medieval world picture. Its first documented appearance is in Camille Flammarion's 1888 book *L'atmosphère: météorologie populaire*, and it has been widely circulated.

3 Two concise articles especially capture Bion's clinical position. They are found in the collection by Bott Spillius, *Melanie Klein Today: Mainly Theory*: "Differentiation of the Psychotic from the Non-Psychotic Personalities" (61–80); and "A Theory of Thinking" (178–86).

4 Tele-technologies feature often in the psychoanalysis of psychotic patients, as one might expect. Herbert Rosenfeld's "Projective Identification in Psychosis" (1971) includes an especially harrowing

account of a patient who experienced being "pulled inside the television" during the Mexican Olympics, to the extent of becoming fused with the situations depicted: "He complained that he was drawn into the hot climate of Mexico which made him feel that being there would make him well. He was also compelled to look at the athletes, or wrestlers and weightlifters and felt he was, or ought to be, one of them. He asked me questions: Why do I have to be an athlete? Why can't I be myself?" (130).

References

Baudrillard, Jean (1994) *Simulacra and Simulation*. Trans. Sheila Glaser. Ann Arbor, MI: University of Michigan Press.

Baudrillard, Jean (1996) *The System of Objects*. Trans. James Benedict. London: Verso.

Baudrillard, Jean (2005) *The Intelligence of Evil or the Lucidity Pact*. Trans. Chris Turner. Oxford: Berg.

Bion, Wilfred (1988a) "Differentiation of the Psychotic from the Non-Psychotic Personalities," in: E. Bott Spillius (ed.) *Melanie Klein Today: Mainly Theory*. pp. 61–80. London: Routledge.

Bion, Wilfred (1988b) "A Theory of Thinking," in: E. Bott Spillius (ed.) *Melanie Klein Today: Mainly Theory*. pp. 178–186. London: Routledge.

Bion, Wilfred (2005) *The Tavistock Seminars*. Francesca Bion (ed.). London: Karnac.

Rosenfeld, Herbert (1971 [1988]) "The Importance of Projective Identification in the Ego Structure and the Object Relations of the Psychotic Patient," in: E. Bott Spillius (ed.) *Melanie Klein Today: Mainly Theory*. pp. 117–137. London: Routledge.

8

*Some Reflections on Baudrillard's "On Disappearance"**

Douglas Kellner

Baudrillard's "On Disappearance" deals with a fundamental dialectic of his work between appearance and disappearance, and alludes to some of his strongest and most distinctive ideas – the disappearance of the real, the subject, and the human being itself in a world of simulation, hyperreality, virtual reality, networks, and the system of what Baudrillard calls "Integral Reality." It would be a mistake to psychologically trivialize this important text to the event of Baudrillard taking leave of us before he disappears, although some passages reasonably allude to the disappearance of a thinker, an idea, or a theory, and its occult afterlife, clearly something now happening with Baudrillard as we ponder "On Disappearance," his legacy, and his difficult to penetrate, but not impenetrable, thought.

Baudrillard opens with a dramatic invocation: "Let us speak then of the world from which human beings have disappeared." This fatal process began, he suggests, "with the disappearance of the real." Citing Hannah Arendt's notion that the "real world" began with the invention of an Archimedean point outside the world – the telescope and modern mathematical calculation (p. 1) – Baudrillard implies that scientific knowledge began with a subject/object dichotomy in which the subject dominates the object with concepts, scientific laws, and theories.

Baudrillard paradoxically suggests that the real vanishes into a concept and that once it is named, it loses its energy, noting: "By representing things to ourselves, by naming them and conceptualizing them, human beings call them into existence and at the same time hasten their doom, subtly detach them from their primal reality" (p. 2). Marx's class struggle becomes a slogan and piece of intellectual history; Freud's Unconscious becomes a cliché and part of an intellectual and business apparatus of psychoanalysis; and globalization becomes a marketing slogan or new form of evil for its opponents. Hence, while for Heidegger and others language creates a world and brings it into being, for Baudrillard theoretical language freezes and reifies the world and begins a process of draining the real into concepts.

In *The Perfect Crime* (1996 [1995]),[1] Baudrillard argues that "reality" in the current media and technological society is disappearing in a "perfect crime," which involves the "destruction of the real." In a world of appearance, image, illusion, virtuality, and hyperreality, where it is no longer possible to distinguish between the virtual and the real, Baudrillard suggests that reality disappears, although its traces continue to nourish an illusion of the real. Just as meaning imploded into the media in his 1970s work, so in the 1990s work reality too imploded into the worlds of the media, computers, and virtuality.

The disappearance of the real through the human project of the domination of the object by the subject leads inexorably in Baudrillard's logic to the disappearance of the human and the subject itself. As the human beings produce a world of astonishing objects, even attempting to clone themselves and postpone or overcome death, the inhuman object world overpowers the subject and its agency, so that "the subject as agency of will, of freedom, or representation; the subject of power, of knowledge, of history – is disappearing" (p. 6).[2]

The "great disappearance" includes the distinctive features of the modern world, its most valued activities such as art, politics, and religion. Baudrillard has long valorized an "art of disappearance,"[3] referring as an example to photography capturing the singularity of the object, devoid of subjectivity, in an emptiness, grasping the delicacy of the world outside of art, ideology, reality, and subjectivity. Yet over the past decade, he has increasingly spoken of the disappearance of art into the world, losing its realm of autonomy and specificity.[4] Likewise, he sees politics and religion as imploding into the world, citing Cardinal Ratzinger (now Pope)'s warning that a "religion which accommodates to the world, which attunes itself to the (political, social . . .) world, becomes superfluous. It is for the same reason – because it became increasingly merged with objective banality – that art [and politics – DK], ceasing to be different from life became superfluous" (pp. 6–7).

And yet, paradoxically, Baudrillard suggests that "everything that disappears – institutions, values, prohibitions, ideologies, even ideas – continues to lead a clandestine existence and exert an occult influence" (pp. 5–6). The subject disappears, but leaves ghosts, fragments, and remains behind. The "end-of-the-world-subjectivity" itself is a "diffuse, floating . . . ectoplasm" that envelops everything, but no longer has an object, reality, or world to stand over against as it has disappeared into this world (p. 6).

I read "On Disappearance" as a pedagogical heuristic to reflect on what has disappeared, what is no longer and no more, such as our modern concepts of reality, meaning, the subject, the social, or those autonomous domains of modernity such as art, politics, religion, or sexuality. Their disappearance, he tells us in this enigmatic meditation, is not the result of an evolutionary process, but is a "singular event . . . which is not negative at all" (p. 4).

Baudrillard is a theorist of break and rupture whose thought grasps fundamental changes and novelties in the contemporary era.[5] While there are sometimes overtones of a messianic and apocalyptic vision in his work, his is not a utopian one. For more conventionally utopian thinkers, an "event" is a positive rupture in history where something new appears, where possibilities emerge, where utopia shines. For Baudrillard, by contrast, the event can signal the disappearance of something important and fundamental – like reality, the world, art, politics, and the human itself. And yet he is not a nihilistic thinker as there are liberatory moments and possibilities in the leaving behind and disappearance of the old and advent of the new, so, at bottom, disappearance "is not negative at all."

Just as Baudrillard's early work on modernity predicates a break between modern and premodern societies,[6] so too does his post-mid-1970s work until his death posit a break between modern societies and something new that has been called by some "the postmodern," although many Baudrillard cadres have trouble enunciating the word and do everything possible to protect Baudrillard from contamination from this unspeakable rupture. And yet Baudrillard constantly posits epochal ruptures – between premodern and modern societies and between modern and postmodern ones, most pronouncedly perhaps in *Symbolic Exchange and Death* and "The Ecstasy of Communication." I would suggest that "On Disappearance" can be read in this register. For Baudrillard is talking of the end and disappearance of the key concepts and domains of the modern era and the entrance into a new conceptual and social space. Thus, in what appeared as his last major text before his death, Baudrillard tells us not only to pay attention to what is new and different in our contemporary moment, but also to reflect on what has disappeared.

Hence, Baudrillard's Big Ideas concern rupture and disappearance.[7] The rupture between modern, premodern, and postmodern animated much of his thought since the 1970s, and with rupture and novelty comes disappearance – as well as reversibility, radical uncertainty, and the need for new oppositional modes of thought and writing. If the era of production has been replaced by an era of simulation and seduction, then the terrain of critique has been supplanted from the real to the symbolic and the imaginary. If the rupture has occurred or is occurring, we are in a situation of reversal and radical uncertainty.[8] Situating oneself in a terrain beyond rupture and in radical uncertainty requires reflection on what is disappearing and what has already disappeared. Thus, his text "On Disappearance" can be situated in the constellation of his key ideas and used to reflect anew on Baudrillard's legacy. Let us, then, carry on the work of mourning by thinking anew Baudrillard's key thoughts and the constellation in which they emerged and continue to live.

Notes

1 See Jean Baudrillard, *The Perfect Crime*. London and New York: Verso Books, 1996.
2 On Baudrillard's metaphysical scenario of the triumph of the object

over subject and displacing of the subject to which he is alluding here, see Douglas Kellner, *Jean Baudrillard: From Marxism to Postmodernism and Beyond*. Cambridge and Palo Alto: Polity Press and Stanford University Press, 1989; and "Jean Baudrillard After Modernity: Provocations On A Provocateur and Challenger," *International Journal of Baudrillard Studies*, 3, 1 (January 2006) at http://www.ubishops.ca/baudrillardstudies/vol3_1/kellner.htm.

3 See Jean Baudrillard, "The Art of Disappearance," in Nicholas Zurbrugg (ed.), *Art and Artefact*. London: Sage, 1997, pp. 28–31.

4 On Baudrillard and the end of art, see my article "Baudrillard and the Art Conspiracy," in *Jean Baudrillard Fatal Theories*, ed. D.B. Clark, M.A. Doel, William Merrin, and R.G. Smith. London and New York: Routledge, 2009: 91–104.

5 On Baudrillard and rupture, see Kellner, *Jean Baudrillard*, op. cit. and "Jean Baudrillard after Modernity," op. cit.

6 See the discussion in the sources in Note 1.

7 Compare Gerry Coulter, "Reversibility: Baudrillard's 'One Great Thought,'" *International Journal of Baudrillard Studies*, 1, 2 (July 2004) at http://www.ubishops.ca/BaudrillardStudies/vol1_2/coulter.htm. I would suggest that rupture and disappearance are connected with reversibility, as in the reversal between a modern era of production and that of simulation, which Baudrillard signals with an evocative "the end . . ." (of political economy, of labor as organizing principle of society, and so on). When a rupture occurs and things disappear one enters inevitably into a scene of reversal and implosion as when alienation is reversed by the "ecstasy of communication," the production and proliferation of meaning and information turn into non-sense and noise, the sovereignty of the subject is displaced by the object, or when the real turns out to be an illusion and illusion and the symbolic give us more illuminating perspectives on the world. Hence, perhaps Baudrillard appears in his afterlife as a Trinitarian with Three Great Thoughts: rupture, disappearance, and reversibility. Or, as I suggest in the text above, a shifting, open, and complex constellation.

8 Here I tip my hat to Mike Gane whose book *Jean Baudrillard: In Radical Uncertainty* (London: Pluto Press, 2000) privileges "radical uncertainty" as a key Baudrillardian idea. I am suggesting here that there is a constellation of fundamental Baudrillardian ideas and want to nominate rupture and disappearance as important parts of the mix.

9

Humanity's End

John Phillips

Humanity's end

Jean Baudrillard returns near the end of his life to a question that underlies all his writings, the question of the human race, its fate, its intelligence and its end: "the human race," he writes, "owes its becoming (and perhaps even its survival) entirely to the fact that it had no end in itself, and certainly not that of becoming what it is (of fulfilling itself, identifying with itself)" (*Intelligence of Evil*, 212). It is a statement of history concerning the human race. It is a complex proposition despite being put in a disarmingly simple way. The history of the human race, first of all, is to be regarded as a *becoming*. He deliberately does not say *being* or *essence*. Yet it is a statement of some kind of negative *essence*. The *essence* of the human race is predicated of negative properties. From its beginning, the human race "had no end." The race now faces its end insofar as it may not be able to "have no end in itself" for much longer. This negation is not dialectical. The *becoming* has no possible correspondence with *being*; unless it is by its *death*. The end of humanity (its purpose, if it had one) is, therefore, the end of humanity (its death). The end of the human race is the end of the human race.

Having no end in Baudrillard's formula is not something one can take for granted. First of all, it requires a persistent strategy mobilized against historical trends whose aims seem to be those of finalizing or finishing off. The present position of the human race, as it faces up to the challenge of the future and to the question of where it might be going, is largely determined by various kinds of end. Ends are always demanded in whatever one sets out to do. An end can be demanded in the form of a purpose, an aim, an objective or even just a deadline. And ends like these are demanded as much by the modes of resistance and revolution (whether democratic, minority, religious, or militant) as by the positivity of those sciences funded by military or economic powers and held in reserve for the arbitrary politics of their operations. An "end" might be given in the register of struggle, or as an alternative to the dominant power, in the form of a *people*, a *postcolonial* identity, or a reactive *cause*. In a telling example, the thousands in Europe who demonstrated with no effect against the war in Iraq using the slogan "not in our name" inevitably evoke an identity and an end and so in this way cannot be distinguished from the powers they would oppose.

Nevertheless, Baudrillard's statements about the end of humanity are deceptively complex. The human race survives and continues to become only so long as it remains true that "it has no end in itself." This is not merely a question of purposes, of aims and objectives. Perhaps after all there's no harm in having a few aims. The proposition concerns *the end* in its element as end *in itself*. It taps into a German philosophical tradition that acknowledges its own roots, via the Latin, amongst the ancient Greeks. Baudrillard has coined here a statement that emerges as the paradoxical negation of a classical dialectic. The "end in itself," the *Ansich* (*potentia, dúnamis*) was always the uncompleted "not yet" of the *Fürsich* (*actus, enérgeia*). The "in itself" was always related to a "for itself." G. W. F. Hegel puts it most clearly in his *Lectures on The History of Philosophy*: "there must be something which is developed, and so something hidden – the seed, the capacity, the potentiality; it is what Aristotle calls *dúnamis*, i.e. possibility, or what is called the *Ansich*, what is *in* itself, and at first only so" (71–72). This *Ansich* performs in traditional thought – especially in its theological forms

– as a kind of *truth*, in the sense of the hidden, necessary, essential *truth* of something (God or the world). To know these things *in themselves* conventionally would be to know them as they really are.

Hegel, in line with most of metaphysics (we'd find the same pattern in Aristotle), does not accept this notion of *Ansich* as *truth*. Hegel's notion of truth implies that something that is merely "in itself" is *not yet* the truth. *In itself* means *not yet*. Potential for Hegel is true in the abstract: "it is the germ of truth, the capacity for, or potentiality of, the truth" (72). But something merely in itself, something abstract, would not be true in actuality. Hegel's example of the *Ansich* is a seed.

> A seed is simple, almost a point; little is visible in it, even under the microscope. But this simple seed is pregnant with all the qualities of the tree. The seed contains the whole tree, its trunk, branches, leaves, colour, smell, taste, etc. And yet this simple thing, the seed, is not the tree itself, the tree's various qualities do not yet exist. (72)

The seed, as is the case with all examples, is *merely* an example but it does have both peculiar illustrative qualities and a historical privilege that is not merely Western (unlike metaphysics, which is). The *truth* of the seed would be the *tree*. Its truth is what it *becomes*; its *truth* is its *becoming*. Somehow the abstract structure of what a seed is to become (the tree) is inherent in it. The example performs all kinds of interferences (an example is never *mere*). The notion of *seed* belongs in the philosophy of nature to the masculine, active, living side of things and tends to be opposed to what is feminine and passionate, and fundamentally, of course, it comes to be opposed to *death*. The idea is that a potential includes within itself the power to become (potential and power are of course synonymous). But in this case, the *power to become* is reduced to the power to become only what it is in actuality (a tree). This is Hegel's characteristic fudging of teleology: something that is *not yet* is nonetheless *already* in an abstract sense. In this case, in other words, the seed cannot choose to become anything but a tree.

Hegel tends not to stray too far from the implications of his arboreal example, when outlining what he thinks of as the actual

content of the dialectic (unfolding history, spirit, logic, conscious-
ness, society, nature, art, etc.). It might seem as if the example
– already as an abstraction – has in some way determined its actualization in the world of Hegel's philosophy. The example serves as
an abstraction – a little fiction or idea – that only becomes true in
the unfolding of history (the history of philosophy and its relation
to the world). The history of philosophy, in Hegel's long lecture
courses, unfolds exactly as if it was a tree, with its seeds in ancient
Greece, and its full leafy crown unfolding in its actuality in German
idealism.

This dialectical law implies that what is *not yet actually* is nonetheless *already* in the abstract. It implies a determination *in advance*
of the *potential* or *power of becoming*. When earlier in his career
Baudrillard turns to Karl Marx and Ferdinand de Saussure he finds
this exact law at work in each of their separate fields, that of production and that of the sign respectively. Yet, in Saussure particularly,
the *potential* can be seen to be operating quite arbitrarily in relation
to anything that it is supposed to *become*. The truth of the sign is
its *arbitrariness* in relation to what it designates. Abstractions can
be produced quite independently of their ability to become real
or to refer to any actuality. One can bring this fact back to Hegel,
who has the virtue of outlining at least in its abstract form the law
of its operation. What would he have made of a seed that was not
answerable to any shape or form inherent already in it? One must
make a distinction before answering. When I say "it might rain
tomorrow" I evoke a real possibility. When I say, however, in one
of Hegel's examples, "the sultan might become pope," I evoke
possibility only superficially (hell freezing over and pigs flying are
typical idioms of superficial possibility). The distinction that Hegel
clings to between "real" potential and "superficial" potential does
not counter the fact that a spurious or superficial potential might
always *become* real historically. No doubt there will be finite constraints that accidentally or contingently allow certain possibilities
whilst making others less accessible. Nevertheless the idea of a seed
that accidentally and by chance determines the shape of its truth,
and of what it becomes, will have serious implications for us.

Hegel's dialectical law exemplified by the seed and the tree must
be regarded as itself something like a potential. Quite independently

of whether it is a spurious fiction or a real possibility it *becomes* real in the dialectics of production and consumption and of the sign and the real. Apparently both Marx and de Saussure unfold their theories in ways that are appropriate for their time, the so-called classical age of Capital and Value. What we witness here is indeed a *force*: the force of a law that has purchase both theoretically and historically. But this *force*, which was supposed to take the form of determinism (it was supposed to become something like a tree), seems no longer attached as potential to anything that would determine it. Hegel uses the term "force," which normally belongs to the natural domain, to refer as he says "analogically" to domains of *ethics* and *politics*. The *force* should be regarded as "an objective counterpart of the activity of *understanding*" (*Phenomenology*, 179). For an extended discussion of the concept of force see John Phillips, "Physics and Formal Adventure: From Aristotle to Heidegger with Hegel and Derrida." *Parallax*, Vol. 15 Issue 2 (May 2009) 4–14, p. 167 line 8. Force should have been the expression of a *mind*. To grasp what is at stake here one needs to remove both the notion of *force* and the structure of *becoming* from the determinism that, in the example of the seed, promises at least a measure of orderly unfolding.

One can, like Deleuze and Guattari, always substitute for *tree* the notion of *rhizome* or of *grass*. This has the virtue of holding onto *nature* for generating political and ethical analogies. The rhizome, though, is still a kind of tree and the less regimented appearance, in terms of its multiple nodes of tuberous growth, remains at best an analogical alternative. It's still a kind of growth. Baudrillard offers something quite different. Let's look again at the proposition I began with: "The human race owes its becoming (and perhaps even its survival) entirely to the fact that it had no end in itself, and certainly not that of becoming what it is (of fulfilling itself, identifying with itself)" (*Intelligence of Evil*, 212). No *essence* and no *identity*: the human race, in this formulation, becomes *arbitrarily*. Its *Ansich* is not related in any necessary or natural way to its *Fürsich*. Two implications follow: first, this is what the state of the human race always is and always has been, it is its principle; and second, the present historical state of *being* (if we are doomed) or *becoming* (if we're lucky) depends entirely on the ways in which this *principle* is conceived and *activated*. Baudrillard's consistent message is that the *principle* of *Ansich* with no relation to *Fürsich* has gathered a momentum powerful enough to mobilize this, its own *force*, against itself. Hence the *Ansich* of the human race is everywhere hounded and attacked in the image – abstraction itself – of a spurious and superficial *Fürsich*: a fictional *activity*, a fictional *determination*, and a fictional *intelligence*.

This fictional intelligence is a simulation of a real intelligence; but only to the extent that it operates according to an imperative that must at all costs deny the source of intelligence *in* simulation. *Simulation* and *intelligence* are expressions of the same force. A *simulated* intelligence though denies its source in the force of simulation. Baudrillard understands history, as if in a technical revision of Hegel's teleology, as the intensification over hundreds of years of the domination in Western societies of spurious and superficial abstractions that stand in for reality. He describes this intensification in terms of "successive mutations of the law of value." Here we may recognize a kind of abstraction that can acknowledge its own force of simulation. Baudrillard's brand of simulation is produced, with meticulous attention to the details of historical becoming, in order to combat an overwhelming trend, which seems mobilized to reduce the forces of simulation or to deny them even as it manifests those forces to the greatest imaginable extent.

Theater of simulation

From the late 1960s Baudrillard had begun to expose and to analyze systems of abstraction powerful enough to *signify* reality and thus to produce a *spurious real*. An abstraction, like the privileged one, *functionality*, is produced by connotation. That is, something does not have to actually have a function in order for it to *connote* functionality. A technical innovation, for instance, can *connote* technical autonomy while actually reducing it. The actually more autonomous system that has been replaced is now experienced as a nostalgic throwback to a primitive past.

One only has to consider the dominant abstractions of our age, like *identity*, *autonomy*, and *integrity*, for the signs and objects that connote these abstractions to emerge in a confusing plurality. The world becomes more complicated with increased capacity for disaster while simultaneously appearing simpler with a connoted increase in the individual's convenience of use. Our environment is increasingly constructed of signs and objects that, while having no essential function, connote functionality. Moreover these objects address us in a certain way. My television, my computer, my iPod, my mobile phone, MySpace, YouTube: each of these objects flatters me and, in an extension of the main function of advertising, assures me that *they* are interested enough in me and my desires to court my attention and participation. Yet these forms of personalization in fact serve the abstraction of automatism in objects: "Automatism," Baudrillard argues in *The System of Objects*, "is simply personalization dreamt in terms of the object" (121).

Baudrillard's development of the logic of simulacra begins with these analyses of abstractions that help produce the cultural and imaginary environments of modern life, but there is considerably more at stake. The *hyperreal*, as he calls it, is an environment in which dialogue, opposition, resistance, negotiation, and all such interactions can be *simulated*. A *simulacrum* in its ordinary sense is straightforwardly an image or semblance of something, rather than the thing itself. And so to simulate something is to assume a false appearance. The connotations of counterfeit and mimicry come together with the military functionality of simulated operation: flight simulators or simulations of battle. Baudrillard's most serious, and most controversial, challenge to political thought is posed in his suggestion that the *Realpolitik* of today's wars involves the functionality of a simulated operation in the connoted guise of the real, and at the cost as we know of hundreds of thousands of human lives.

Nevertheless we should guard against taking the arguments about simulacra too literally. We can establish a bit of distance once we observe that there was never an alternative to simulation of some kind. It is not as if simulation has taken over *from* a previously existing *real*. The real, in other words, which is what we mean by the ways things, objects, and individuals *appear*, would always have been a function of some kind of *mediation*, which is where the *force* of self-activating potential resides. So to establish the premises

on which his arguments are made, Baudrillard tends to divide his
terms up into orders, phases, or stages, which each time designate
progressive changes in how things appear. What he calls the "three
orders of simulacra" are glossed as "orders of appearance." He puts
it this way:

> Three orders of appearance, parallel to the mutations of the law of
> value, have followed one another since the Renaissance:
>   – *Counterfeit* is the dominant scheme of the "classical" period, from
> the Renaissance to the industrial revolution;
>   – *Production* is the dominant scheme of the industrial era;
>   – *Simulation* is the reigning scheme of the current phase that is con-
> trolled by the code.
>   The first order of simulacrum is based on the natural law of value,
> that of the second order on the commercial law of value, that of the
> third order on the structural law of value. (*Simulations*, 83)

Baudrillard's arguments are attempts to make a difference to
how we think about the frameworks that govern our thoughts and
actions. This hypothetical schema functions as a kind of *game* but is
based on fairly stable principles. The historical trajectory is matched
by the logic of paradoxically circular progression. The progression
meets its limit each time an internal reversibility asserts itself. It's
not a matter of preferring a Renaissance culture over the present,
but the first order of simulacra leaves the most room, according
to Baudrillard, for "a critical or ideal projection" (*Simulacra*, 121).
The progression that Baudrillard charts is the reverse of most ideas
of modern progress, but there's little sense of nostalgia. Rather
than recover some spurious idea of Renaissance value (the natural
law of value) Baudrillard tends to mobilize the counterfeit itself
and thus to deploy forms of simulation *against* the simulated codes
of present reality.

The Renaissance scheme, he argues, is that of theatricality.
Theatricality is exactly what the *obscenity* of contemporary media
seems to want to destroy, in its drive to make everything transparent: "Obscenity begins," Baudrillard says in *The Ecstasy of
Communication*, "when there is no more spectacle, no more stage,
no more theatre, no more illusions, when everything becomes

immediately transparent" (*Ecstasy*, 21). The process of obscenity, then, begins during the European Renaissance as the theater stage is oriented more and more to representations.

One can test this out independently. Pico della Mirandola's so-called "Oration: on the Dignity of Man" begins by establishing mankind as the most privileged of all beings because he has no essence in himself. He has no end in himself and is distinguished only by a capacity for imitation. In this way he can become beast or even plant but he also can become angel or, by learning the fundamentally secret arts, something like a God. There is an illustration from Robert Fludd's *Utriusque cosmi – historia* from 1617, which belongs within the same tradition that placed man – as actor and operator – in the center of the Ptolemaic cosmic structure. A monkey sits on the earth, which is at the lowest and most central point of the cosmos. The monkey is tied by a chain held by the figure of a woman hovering over him, and who represents the entire celestial world: sun, moon, planets and fixed stars. These last represent the Zodiac. Three outer spheres inhabited by angelic figures lead up ultimately to the Deity (hidden behind clouds of

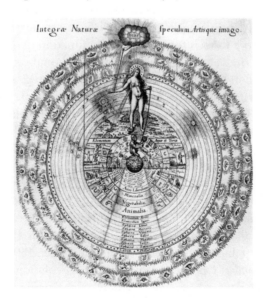

From Robert Fludd, Utriusque cosmi – historia *[I.3] 1617*
(© Bettman Corbis)

glory and named in Hebrew), to which is linked the woman figure by another chain. The monkey owing to its imitative capacities represents Man's artistic faculties – a greater power, as Pico had insisted in his "Oration," than "Dignity."

Knowledge of nature is thus achieved through imitation of it, which also allows Man to reproduce and thus obtain its powers. The conceit is that of Man's ability to discover, imitate and learn to manipulate the entire chain of being. Mankind in this first order of simulation already is the pure simulacrum. Nonetheless, in taking his distance from nature, he is capable of projecting a wild and secret utopia that strives towards the transcendent.

The theatrical simulacrum, in Baudrillard's scheme, is eventually absorbed by the second order, the order of production, which is in fact always a form of reproduction in signs that incessantly signify their own productivity. It is not difficult in the age of post-colonial theory to recognize the workings of a second order that pursues the aims of globalization and expansion by materializing force through the development of the machine, but which has in turn been further absorbed by the age of simulation, in which we find ourselves today, only a few years after Baudrillard's death.

Baudrillard's challenge is not so much aimed at the great Western powers, whose force is for him entirely a function of the hyperreal itself, but at the status of knowledge and the thought that produces it. The relationship of thought, and thus of learning, is connected in the deepest possible way to his analyses of simulacra and simulation. In this respect he returns us to historically very old patterns of struggle over the stakes and modes of knowledge and belief.

The place of the sun in contemporary discourses operates as a powerful analogue for Baudrillard to the extent that a false or counterfeit power, which had once been symbolized by the illuminating power of this brightest star, has now by connotation passed to the abstract notion of the *people*. Baudrillard refers to this movement as "a Copernican revolution in reverse." In 1543 Nicolas Copernicus published his treatise (written between 1507 and 1530) *De Revolutionibus Orbium Coelestium* (The Revolution of Celestial Spheres) where the heliocentric model of the world is presented for the first time, displacing "Man" from the center of the earlier classical and medieval schemas. He had written:

In the middle of all dwells the Sun. Who indeed in this most beautiful temple would place the torch in any other or better place than one whence it can illuminate the whole at the same time? Not ineptly, some call it the lamp of the universe, others its mind, others again its ruler – Trismegistus, the visible God, Sophocles' Electra, the contemplation of all things. (Copernicus)

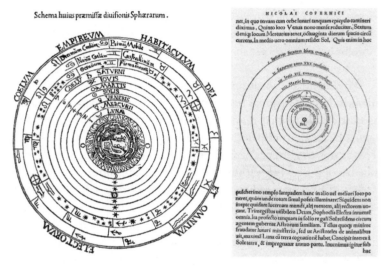

Ptolemaic Model of the Universe   Heliocentric Model of the Universe

A Copernican revolution in reverse, as the following quotation from "The Precession of Simulacra" confirms, does not simply return us to a dark age; but rather it fulfills the movement, it completes the revolution supposedly established by Copernicus in the sixteenth century, of reducing to nothing the gap between knowledge and the unknowable, between perception and its unperceivable origin.

The simulacrum of the inversion or the involution of poles, this clever subterfuge, which is the secret of the whole discourse of manipulation and thus, today, in every domain, the secret of any new power in the erasure of the scene of power, in the assumption of all words from which has resulted this fantastic silent majority characteristic of our time – all of this started without a doubt in the political sphere with the democratic simulacrum, which today is the substitution for the power of God with the power of the people as the source of power, and of power as *emanation* with power as *representation*. Anti-Copernican revolution: no transcendental instance either of the sun or of the luminous source of power and knowledge – everything comes from the people and everything returns to them. It is with this magnificent recycling that the universal simulacrum of manipulation, from the scenario of mass suffrage to the present-day phantoms of opinion polls, begins to be put in place. (*Simulacra and Simulation*, 42)

Baudrillard's evocation of the endlessness of mankind – of mankind as an-original becoming – is thus an attempt to conjure, against the drive that renders everything transparent, a source that *cannot* be made transparent: the source of seduction, of the secret. This is not to evoke a notion of the real to which the simulacrum can be opposed but rather it is to affirm the difference between orders of simulacra, in transitional phases during which simulacra can be revealed for what they are.

When reading Baudrillard, it is not possible to avoid the sense that we members of the twenty-first century are unlucky to live in a world dominated by the drive for completion, and which attacks us on multiple levels. Nonetheless Baudrillard can best be characterized, alongside his eternal vigilance against completion, by his affirmation of the essential indeterminacy of a future whose becoming belongs to an irreducible "in itself," a potential that knows no end. In a world whose business it is to anticipate the future we should expect monsters; but to affirm the chance of an indeterminate future is to welcome that possibility.

References

Baudrillard, Jean (1983) *Simulations*. Trans. Paul Foss et al. New York: Semiotext[e].

Baudrillard, Jean (1988) *The Ecstasy of Communication*. Trans. Bernard and Caroline Schutze. New York: Semiotext[e].

Baudrillard, Jean (1994) *Simulacra and Simulation*. Trans. Sheila Glaser. Ann Arbor, MI: University of Michigan Press.

Baudrillard, Jean (1996) *The System of Objects*. Trans. James Benedict. London: Verso.

Baudrillard, Jean (2005) *The Intelligence of Evil or the Lucidity Pact*. Trans. Chris Turner. Oxford: Berg.

Fludd, Robert (1987) *The Origin and Structure of the Cosmos*. Trans. Patricia Tahil. Edinburgh: Magnum Opus Hermetic Sourceworks No. 13.

Fludd, Robert (2001) *Selections*. William Huffman (ed.). Berkeley, CA: North Atlantic Books.

Hegel, G. W. F. (1977) *Phenomenology of Spirit*. Trans. A. V. Miller. Oxford: Oxford University Press.

Hegel, G. W. F. (1985) *Introduction to the Lectures on the History of Philosophy*. Trans. T. M. Knox and A. V. Miller. Oxford: Clarendon.

Pico della Mirandola (1965) *On the Dignity of Man*. Trans. Charles Glen Wallis. Indianapolis, IN: Hackett.

Index

Note: page references in *italics* indicate illustrations

Index